TOM STANDAGE is deputy editor of *The Economist* and the author of seven books, including *A History of the World in 6 Glasses*. His writing has also appeared in the *New York Times*, the *Daily Telegraph*, the *Guardian* and *Wired*. *Oddly Informative* is the sequel to *Go Figure*, *Seriously Curious*, *Uncommon Knowledge*, *Unconventional Wisdom* and *Truly Peculiar*, also edited by him.

ODDLY INFORMATIVE

Matters of FACT THAT AMAZE and DELIGHT

EDITED BY
TOM STANDAGE

The
Economist

Published in 2022 under exclusive licence from The Economist by
Profile Books Ltd
29 Cloth Fair
London EC1A 7JQ
www.profilebooks.com

Typeset in Milo by MacGuru Ltd

Printed and bound in Great Britain by CPI Group (UK) Ltd, Croydon CR0 4YY

A CIP catalogue record for this book is available from the British Library

ISBN 978 1 80081 209 3
eISBN 978 1 80081 210 9

Contents

Introduction: why unusual explanations can be oddly informative

HUMAN BRAINS ARE storytelling machines. In the words of the psychologist Jonathan Haidt, "the human mind is a story processor, not a logic processor". Stories help us understand and help us remember. Human knowledge has long been passed down in the form of stories, and it still is. Go to a conference or a dinner party, and it's the unexpected and amusing stories and anecdotes, not dry facts and figures, that you will find easiest to recall afterwards. Something about the shape of an unusual story makes it lodge in our brains.

All of which suggests that a good way to learn, understand and remember more about the way the world works is to focus on the collection and consumption of unusual narratives. That is where this book comes in. We have done the first – gathering curious explanations, facts and figures from *The Economist*'s output of explainers and daily charts, all of which illuminate the world in unexpected ways – so that you can do the second, and feast on freakishly fascinating facts.

Did you know, for example, that couples are more likely to divorce if their first child is a girl? Or that the idea of daylight saving time was mooted by Benjamin Franklin, but only caught on in the first world war? Or that a state in Mexico has an all-female traffic-police unit, because women are less likely to be corrupt than men? Or that there are equine equivalents of economy, business and first class when transporting racehorses on planes? Or that there are fairer ways to run penalty shoot-outs in football, but nobody wants to use them because they are too confusing?

The oddness of such stories makes them entertaining. But it also makes them more likely to stick in your head, so you retain them – and the insights and understanding they often encapsulate. The story of the sports boycott against apartheid South Africa explains why some boycotts work, and others don't, for example. The tales of Australia's mouse plague, and of America's "Brood X" cicadas, cast light on population dynamics and the fight between predator and prey. The account of what really doomed electric cars in the early 20th century illustrates what must be done to encourage their adoption in the 21st. And so on.

Strange though they may be, such explanations can, in short, be unusually enlightening – or, to put it another way, oddly informative. We hope you will enjoy reading them – and remembering them.

Tom Standage
Deputy Editor, *The Economist*
July 2022

Oddly informative: matters of fact that amaze and delight

Why having daughters rather than sons makes divorce more likely

Daughters have long been linked with divorce. Several studies conducted in America since the 1980s provide strong evidence that a couple's first-born being a girl increases the likelihood that they will subsequently split up. At the time, the researchers involved speculated that this was an expression of "son preference", a phenomenon which, in its most extreme form, manifests itself as the selective abortion or infanticide of female offspring.

Work published in 2020 in the *Economic Journal*, however, debunks that particular idea. In "Daughters and Divorce", Jan Kabatek of the University of Melbourne and David Ribar of Georgia State University, in Atlanta, confirm that having a female first-born does indeed increase the risk of that child's parents divorcing, in both America and the Netherlands. But, unlike previous work, their study also looked at the effect of the girl's age. It found that "daughter-divorce" risk emerges only in a first-born girl's teenage years. Before they reach the age of 12, daughters are no more linked to couples splitting up than sons are. "If fathers were really more likely to take off because they preferred sons, surely they wouldn't wait 13 years to do so," reasons Dr Kabatek. Instead, he argues, the fact that the risk is so age-specific requires a different explanation – namely, that parents quarrel more over the upbringing of teenage daughters than of teenage sons.

Taken over the years, the daughter effect, though real, is small. In the Netherlands, for example, by the time their first-born is 18, 20.12% of couples will have divorced if that child is a son, compared with 20.48% if she is a daughter – an increase in probability of 1.8%. But in the five years when the first-born is between the ages of 13 and 18, that increase goes up to 5%. And it peaks, at 9%, when the child is 15. In America the figures are roughly double this (but this finding is based on a smaller data set and is therefore less certain).

Anyone who has – or has been – a teenager knows how turbulent those years can be. Surveys confirm that teenage daughters and fathers, in particular, get on each other's nerves. They also show that parents of teenage daughters argue more about parenting than the parents of sons tend to, and that mothers of teenage daughters report significantly more disagreements with their partners over money, and become more open to the idea of divorce. Previous research has also shown that one of the most common things parents fight over is how much they should control their teenagers' personal choices, such as how they dress, whom they date and where they work.

In light of all this, it is intriguing to note that Dr Kabatek and Dr Ribar found one type of couple who seem immune to the daughter effect: those in which the father grew up with a sister. Having seen things somewhat from a sister's point of view may, in short, act as a sort of social inoculation.

Changing the clocks is unpopular. Why do it?

Sometimes the decision to change a country's time zone can be political. Despite its vastness, all of China runs on Beijing time – a decision taken by Mao Zedong in 1949 to instil unity. (Pity the poor people of Xinjiang province in China's far west, where sometimes the sun does not rise until 10am.) For almost three years, until 2018, North Korea existed in its own time zone, half an hour behind its southern neighbour, in keeping with its hermit tendencies. But more often countries fiddle with the time of day for practical reasons. Some 70 countries, mostly in the Americas and Europe, apply daylight saving time during the summer months. But is it necessary?

In the 18th century Benjamin Franklin mooted the idea of moving the clocks forward in the summer. But the practice really took hold during the first world war. Britain, France and Germany calculated that by adding an extra hour's daylight in the evening, a saving could be made on coal. This, in turn, would help the war effort. Later, other benefits suggested themselves. It might increase consumer spending, as shoppers are encouraged to stay out later into the evening. It might even reduce crime. As the ne'er-do-well's adage might go: "the longer the daylight, the less I do wrong."

For all that, clock-changing is unpopular. In 2019 the European Parliament voted to end this long-established practice from 2021 – though the small matter of a global pandemic, and the refusal of the Council of the European Union to endorse the change, have led to the idea being put on hold indefinitely. When the EU ran a poll among its citizens, it gathered nearly 5m responses. Over 80% wanted time-alternating scrapped, and for good reason. Although it has not been proven conclusively, many scientists think that changing the clocks messes with humans' circadian rhythms. It is, says one, akin to injecting a micro-dose of jet lag. This may increase the chances of heart attacks and strokes. It could also be that car accidents increase, as drivers used to commuting in the daylight, for example, suddenly have to do so in the dark (or vice versa). Productivity may go down too. Perhaps most inconvenient for businesses is the fact that countries may change their clocks at different times. That means the time difference between London and New York, say, which is usually five hours, is instead four hours for a few weeks each year, which causes confusion.

With the EU's abolition of clock-changing in limbo, attention has turned to America. Some state legislatures have passed laws to stick with summer time all year round, among them California, Florida and Washington, but a lack of congressional approval means their residents still have to change their clocks. In March 2022 the Senate passed a bill to the same effect – the Sunshine Protection Act, which must still clear the House of Representatives in order to become law. It is the brainchild of Marco Rubio, a senator from the "Sunshine State" of Florida. "Pardon the pun," he said after the bill was approved by the Senate, "but this is an idea whose time has come."

Why Z is for Putin

In Cyrillic, the letter "Z" is written "3". But after Vladimir Putin launched his invasion of Ukraine in February 2022, the Latin form proliferated inside Russia. Just days after the invasion, Maria Butina, a Russian spy-turned-politician, filmed a video of herself drawing a Z on her coat. "Keep it up, brothers," she declared. "We're with you forever." The governor of Kemerovo, a coal-mining region in Siberia unofficially called "Kuzbass" ("Кузбасс"' in Cyrillic), decreed that its name would henceforth be rendered in a Cyrillic-Latin mix as "КуZбасс". Ivan Kuliak, a Russian gymnast, plastered a Z on his uniform when he took the podium beside a Ukrainian competitor at the Gymnastics World Cup in Qatar on March 5th, causing the International Gymnastics Federation to start disciplinary proceedings against him. Why did the letter Z become a symbol of support for Vladimir Putin's war?

As Russian forces assembled along Ukraine's borders in early 2022, sharp-eyed observers of open-source intelligence noticed curious characters painted on the sides of Russian tanks. Among them were the letter V, the letter Z inside a box, and a plain letter Z. The mysterious runes generated myriad theories: perhaps Z was shorthand for "zapad", which means "west" in Russian (the direction Russian forces would be marching); maybe it indicated the Kremlin's desire to take out Ukraine's president, Volodymyr Zelensky. Military analysts instead reckon that the letters correspond to particular parts of the Russian forces involved in the invasion. With more than 100 battalion tactical groups of between 600 and 1,000 troops from as far away as the Russian Far East involved in the invasion of Ukraine, such markings may have helped to distinguish between them and their foes on the battlefield.

Once the fighting began, Russia's state propaganda machine turned the Z into the operation's unofficial logo. Russia's defence ministry suggested that it stands for "za", the Russian word for "for", as in "for victory". RT, a Russian propaganda network, began hawking T-shirts emblazoned with the letter. Vladimir Solovyov, a noxious state television host, plastered it on his laptop. Pro-war graffiti spotted in Ekaterinburg, a mid-sized city on the edge of Siberia, featured the letter prominently. Nationalist activists in Moscow organised a caravan of cars with Zs painted on them to circle the city. A children's hospice in Kazan, a city in western Russia, lined patients up in a Z formation for a photograph. Expressing his support for Mr Putin, the director of the charity that runs the hospice, Vladimir Vavilov, told a local news agency that the "fascist" force in Ukraine, as Mr Putin has labelled the country's democratically elected leadership, "can only be stopped with force, there is no other way, no mercy!"

The Z's adoption several days into the operation suggests that the planning for Russia's information war may have been just as haphazard as the shooting war plans appear to have been. There is a particular irony to making a Latin letter the symbol of a war that Mr Putin has justified in part by spurious claims that the Russian language was under threat in Ukraine. The Z had never been associated with Mr Putin's regime before, and has none of the long-cultivated symbolism of other notorious icons, such as the Nazi swastika, to which Ukraine's defence minister has compared it. Yet the Z has already become a chilling shorthand. Opposition figures and others who have spoken out against the war inside Russia have found the letter scrawled on their apartments; agents from Russia's security services left a Z inside the office of Memorial, a storied human-rights group, after a raid of its premises. Russian officials have adopted it to demonstrate allegiance to their leader. Now, more than anything, Z is for Putin.

Which is the most recognisable country on Google Street View?

Dedicated fans of Google Street View, which lets users explore cities and towns around the world by clicking their way around inside panoramic street-level imagery, have come up with dozens of applications for the tool, from house-hunting to holiday planning to experimental art. The most entertaining use of the service may be "Geoguessr", a game created in 2013 by Anton Wallén, a Swedish IT consultant. The premise of Geoguessr is simple: players are dropped at random places in Google Street View, without any information about their location. They are then scored based on how well they guess where they are, using clues (such as road signs) they can find in the vicinity.

Geoguessr is a fun way to kill time. But it also offers a clever way to determine which parts of the world are the most recognisable, and who can recognise them best. With this in mind, *The Economist* obtained some 1.2m guesses from the online geography quiz, submitted by 223,942 people in 192 countries and territories between January and August 2020. We then used this dataset to compile a "recognisability index" for each country, defined as the share of players who guessed correctly where they were dropped minus the share who guessed incorrectly. (We excluded games in which a player was dropped into his or her own country, and countries that appeared in the dataset fewer than 20,000 times.)

According to our analysis, Japan is by far the most recognisable country. Geoguessr players dropped there correctly guessed their location 64% of the time, whereas those dropped elsewhere incorrectly guessed Japan just 9% of the time. In second place is America, which players guessed correctly 79% of the time and incorrectly 40% of the time. Russia ranks third, followed by Italy, Brazil and Britain (see chart overleaf). As for which countries were most often confused for one another, 18% of players who reckoned they had been dropped in America were actually in Australia. Spain

If you could be anywhere

Player's guess vs Google Street View location in Geoguessr video game
Jan–Oct 2020, top 16 countries

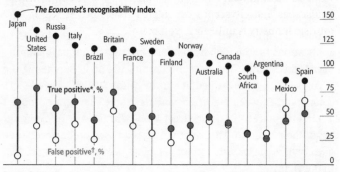

Sources: Geoguessr; *The Economist*

*Players correctly placed themselves

†Players wrongly believed they were in the country when they were elsewhere

and Mexico were also frequently mixed up. Not all the guesses made sense: at least one person mistook Luxembourg for Mongolia.

Germany and Switzerland are home to the best Geoguessr players, followed by France, Belgium and the Netherlands. At the bottom of our list is Turkey, followed by Russia and America, where players correctly guessed their location just 45% of the time. Geoguessr scores do, however, depend on how close the guesser is in kilometres to the right location. If borders are involved, some guessers might score highly even when they plump for the wrong country. So picking Vancouver would give a greater score than New York, if the dropped location was Seattle. Curiously, players in Norway, Sweden and Colombia are better at identifying the country where they are dropped than the precise location. In America, the skills are reversed. Americans score about as well as Brits in figuring out their approximate location but are abysmal at picking the right country.

Such results should be taken with a big pinch of salt. Not all countries are included in Google Street View. Of those that are, many have incomplete coverage. Most streets in Germany, for example, are missing from Google Maps because of privacy concerns; China is also missing, with the exceptions of Macau and Hong Kong. With those caveats, it must still be pleasing to be the country with the landscapes and cityscapes considered most distinctive. Japan's tourism industry is unlikely to complain.

Why do countries move their capital cities?

In 2019 the president of Indonesia, Joko Widodo, unveiled a surprise plan to move the country's capital. In January 2022 he announced that the new capital would be called Nusantara ("archipelago" in Javanese). The new city, estimated to cost $32bn, will sit on 180,000 hectares of what is now jungle on the island of Borneo. Egypt too has ambitions to build a grand new capital. In December 2021 the government held its first cabinet meeting in the as-yet-unnamed new administrative capital, a city being built some 49km east of Cairo. Why do countries change their capital cities?

Historically, rulers have used new capitals to unite different areas. Legend holds that King Menes merged upper and lower Egypt into one kingdom in 3150BC, and placed Memphis at its centre. President George Washington handpicked the location of Washington, DC in 1790 as a bridge between the northern and southern states – though it was a bastion of the Union during the civil war. And Australia chose Canberra as its capital at the start of the 20th century in part because it was roughly equidistant from both Melbourne and Sydney.

Moving the capital does not guarantee unity, however. In 1991 Nigeria moved its capital from Lagos, on the south coast, to Abuja, in the middle of the country. Lagos was historically dominated by the Christian Yoruba, and Abuja was supposed to be a buffer zone between the Christian south and the Muslim north. But the Hausa, the largest Islamic tribe, has benefited most from the move to Abuja. That many of the public buildings in Abuja employ Islamic imagery further rankles Christians. And the indigenous Gwari people, driven off their land to make way for the city, still protest.

Not all moves are well intentioned. Sometimes leaders want to build a stronghold far from their unhappy subjects. Myanmar's capital, Naypyidaw, is a military vanity project, built in 2004 to secure the junta's seat of power. In 2017 President Teodoro Obiang of Equatorial Guinea, Africa's longest-serving dictator, moved the capital from Malabo to Oyala. Having come to power by way of a coup, the president was keen to house himself in a secure place, away from rebels, critics and activists.

Indonesia's president claims to have more noble aims. He promises a zero-emissions paradise and says the move will redistribute wealth, which is heavily concentrated in Western urban areas. Critics counter that much of the land the government is buying up is already owned by wealthy individuals and companies, including mining and logging operations. Brazil tried to do something similar with Brasilia, which replaced Rio de Janeiro as its capital in 1960. The new city was supposed to create an egalitarian society without informal workers or lawless favelas, and to bring some of the wealth of the south-east to the country's poor interior. Instead, the demographics of the city grew to mirror the rest of Brazil. Today it is one of the most unequal cities in the world.

The most compelling reason to move is also the most prosaic: there are often limits to the growth of cities. Jakarta is traffic-clogged, overcrowded and flood-prone. It is also one of the fastest-sinking cities in the world. Moving the capital, and with it the government, civil service and possibly big employers, should alleviate some pressure. But establishing a new capital takes time. After its founding in 1790, Washington, DC was for a long time mocked as a city plan without a city. Even today, it continues to have plenty of detractors.

Why are women less likely to be corrupt than men?

Transparency International, a non-profit group, released its annual report on corruption around the world in January 2022. Measured by its average index, corruption has not improved for a decade. In many poor countries it is getting worse. The authors' recommendations include strengthening anti-corruption agencies, cracking down on financial crime and making public spending more transparent. But some countries have tried a different method: hiring more women. In 2011, for example, a state in Mexico created an all-female traffic-police unit with the aim of stamping out corruption. The number of complaints against traffic police dropped precipitously. In Peru, which took a similar approach in the late 1990s, surveys show that female traffic officers are considered to be stricter and harder to bribe. Are women really less corrupt than men?

The idea gained credence after researchers from the World Bank published a study in 2001 that looked at 100 countries. It found that in those with a greater proportion of female legislators, officials were less likely to demand bribes. More recent research by a group of academics, including Francesco Decarolis of Bocconi University in Milan, came to a similar conclusion. It found that in China between 1979 and 2014, senior female bureaucrats were 81% less likely to have been arrested for corruption than their male colleagues. And in Italy between 2000 and 2016, female officials were 22% less likely than male ones to have been investigated for corruption.

The authors stopped short of proposing a reason for the gap. But other academics, such as Elin Bjarnegard, of Uppsala University in Sweden, have offered possible explanations. One is that female officials tend to have fewer opportunities to take bribes or wield connections improperly. Corruption thrives within "old boys' clubs". It may be that such groups, typically dominated by men, tend to trust and induct people who look like them, keeping women out. Such networks also want to enlist people who have access to money and other resources – again, more likely to be men – which can be used for things such as vote-buying. Evidence from Argentina found that female legislators were less likely than male ones to be part of the large political parties that are most associated with corruption. And in Mexico many women in politics start their careers in NGOs, rather than by working their way up within a corrupt network, so they are less likely to be involved in graft.

Another plausible explanation is that female politicians avoid corruption because they are more severely punished for it. Many voters expect women to conform to the stereotype that they are more honest and compassionate than men. Women who do not match this stereotype pay heavily for it. Such was the case in Malawi in 2014, according to research published in the journal *Women's Studies International Forum*. Using survey data and focus groups, the study found that Joyce Banda, Malawi's president at the time, may have paid a higher price in the polls for a corruption scandal than her male predecessors did for similar transgressions. Higher expectations of propriety may lead women to be more risk-averse than men on average.

These explanations are grounded in the reality that women have less power than men. So any corruption gender gap could fade in countries where the sexes become more equal. This has already been found to be the case for the gender gap in general crime. On average, women still commit fewer offences than men. But women have become more criminal over the past 50 years. That is in part because technological and social progress have allowed them more time to work outside the home (both legally and illegally). Something similar could happen with corruption. As the ranks of female officials grow and they find themselves on an equal footing with men, stereotypes and gender-based scrutiny may weaken. Who knows: women may even start establishing "old girls' clubs".

Why do authoritarian regimes like to buy English football clubs?

Newcastle United holds a tragi-comic place in the minds of English football fans. The club can seemingly make a mess out of any situation. Despite a large and passionate supporter base, it has not won the top division in nearly a century. The last time it came close, in 1996, it blew a 12-point lead and its manager, Kevin Keegan, had a public meltdown after some gentle taunting by Alex Ferguson, his rival at Manchester United. Despite the club's hapless history, in October 2021 a consortium backed by Saudi Arabia's sovereign-wealth fund, which is chaired by Muhammad bin Salman, the kingdom's crown prince, announced it had bought Newcastle United for £305m ($415m). Newcastle thus joined Chelsea and Manchester City as another Premier League team with owners linked to an autocratic government. Why are authoritarian regimes so keen on English football clubs?

One reason is to project soft power. In her book *Putin's People*, Catherine Belton claims that Russia's president directed Roman Abramovich, an oligarch who had become rich under his patronage, to buy Chelsea, a moderately successful west London team. (Mr Abramovich denies this, and sold the club after Russia invaded Ukraine in February 2022.) The Kremlin, says Ms Belton, had decided that the way to gain acceptance in British society was via the country's greatest love: football. "From the start the acquisition had been aimed at building a beach-head for Russian influence in the UK," she writes. Owning a high-profile European club also gives regimes more clout within FIFA, the global game's governing body. That may have proved useful when Russia bid successfully for the 2018 World Cup. The same goes for Qatar, which in 2011 bought Paris St Germain, France's highest-profile side, and subsequently won the right to host the 2022 World Cup – despite many people arguing that a tiny, desert state with a questionable human-rights record was an unsuitable host of the event. Hosting major sporting events is another way for authoritarian countries to project soft power and change how they are perceived abroad.

Human-rights group Amnesty International called the Newcastle deal "a clear attempt by the Saudi authorities to sportswash their appalling human-rights record with the glamour of top-flight football". The NGO cited the country's penchant for locking up and harassing critics, its repression of women and the brutal state-backed murder in 2018 of Jamal Khashoggi, a journalist. But there is also a business case that can be advanced. England is home to the most watched and richest domestic football league in the world. The Premier League's latest deal with broadcasters – clubs' biggest source of revenue – is worth an estimated £3.2bn ($4.4bn) a season, nearly double the €2.1bn ($2.4bn) that Spain's top league brings in. Add in gate receipts, replica-kit sales and the like, and a football team can be a lucrative venture. In 2008 Sheikh Mansour, a member of Abu Dhabi's royal family, is believed to have paid around £150m for Manchester City. The £2bn-plus he is estimated to have since spent on world-class players, coaches and facilities has brought the club five Premier League trophies. In 2019 he sold a smallish stake to a private-equity fund, which valued the whole club at £3.7bn.

With Newcastle added to the growing list of super-wealthy English clubs, buying success will become harder. Clubs are also now somewhat limited by "financial fair play" rules which mean that, in general, they may not spend much more than they earn (although some wealthy owners have found inventive ways around this). The Premier League also bars states from being overly influential within its football clubs. It was this concern that stymied the Saudis' previous bid for Newcastle, in 2020. But the following year the league's concerns were assuaged by "legally binding" assurances that the kingdom would not interfere in the running of the club. When assessing such takeovers, however, ask not what the country can do for the club, but what the club can do for the country.

What is the relationship between religiosity and belief in conspiracy theories?

Americans who believe in the conspiracy theories collectively packaged as "QAnon" gained international notoriety after a large group of them were involved in storming the US Capitol building on January 6th 2021. But the precise cause of the movement's appeal has yet to be pinned down. One theory is that Americans who have no religious affiliation find themselves attracted to other causes instead, such as the QAnon cult. A competing theory, posited by Ben Sasse, a Republican senator from Nebraska, is that modern strains of Christian evangelicalism that "run on dopey apocalypse-mongering" do not entirely satisfy all worshippers – so they go on to find community and salvation in other groups, such as QAnon. So is religiosity associated with a lesser or greater propensity to believe in conspiracy theories?

Using *The Economist*'s polling with online pollster YouGov, it is possible to test both theories. From July 10th to July 13th 2021, YouGov asked Americans about their racial and religious affiliations, whether they thought of QAnon favourably or unfavourably, and whether they believed in a variety of other popular conspiracy theories. Those theories included old standbys, such as whether the Moon landing in 1969 was faked.

According to YouGov's polling, which we combined with a survey from March 2021 to obtain a larger sample size, Americans who attend church the least are also the least likely to have a favourable view of QAnon. Among those who say they "never" go to church, just 9% of those who have heard of the QAnon conspiracy view it favourably. Fully 92% of these respondents view it unfavourably – a net favourability of minus 83 percentage points. But the net favourability rating among people who attend church the most – once a month or more – is minus 52 points.

We ran a statistical model to control for potential links between attitudes towards QAnon and other demographic factors such as race, age, gender, education, party affiliation and vote choice in

Preaching to the choir

United States, attitudes towards QAnon and other conspiracies, July 10th–13th 2021

Share of people who "definitely/probably" believe each theory, % responding

● White evangelicals ○ Everyone else

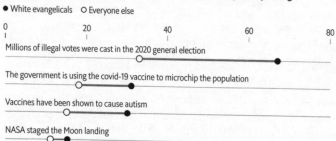

Net favourability* of QAnon, by church attendance, % points†

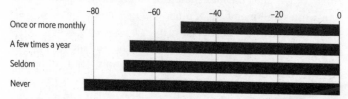

Source: YouGov/*The Economist*

*Among people who said they had heard of QAnon, excluding "don't know"
†Includes data from March 6th–9th 2021

2020. Our model confirmed that the relationship between church attendance and QAnon was not a statistical fluke: adults who attended church at least once a month were still eight percentage points more likely to rate QAnon favourably. White evangelicals, the most religiously devout group among those surveyed by YouGov, are particularly susceptible to supporting QAnon and believing other conspiracy theories. They also tend to attend church frequently. According to YouGov, 22% of evangelicals who know about QAnon view it favourably, compared with 11% among the rest of the adult population. At the other end of the spectrum, 24% of evangelicals rate QAnon as "very unfavourable", compared with 58% among other people.

It is not clear, however, whether those who have a favourable opinion of QAnon do so because they enjoy membership of a like-minded social group, as Mr Sasse and others claim, or merely because they are more susceptible to conspiratorial thinking. For example, 31% of white evangelicals also believe the false theory, popular on social media, that the American government used covid-19 vaccination as an opportunity to insert microchips into Americans – compared with 18% among everyone else. About 30% of white evangelicals believe that vaccines cause autism, which is double the percentage among the rest of the adult population.

Belief in such theories is also linked to a person's political views. White evangelicals are 34 percentage points more likely than other Americans to believe that "millions of illegal votes" were cast in the 2020 election. These adults also tend to be more conservative, and vote for Republican politicians more often, than non-whites and members of other religious groups. Evangelicals are influenced by the official party line on issues of the day – even if they are conspiratorial. And adoption of one wild theory, perhaps made more persuasive by a politician's avowals, tends to lead to the adoption of others. Beliefs are bolstered if held by members of friendship groups. YouGov's polling suggests that conspiratorial thinking is not associated with a dearth of religious fervour. On the contrary, more devout Christians tend to be more credulous when it comes to conspiracies.

Why can't NASA's female astronauts fly as much as men?

Like Earth, space has struggled with equality. When Wally Funk finally made the journey into space aboard Jeff Bezos's New Shepard rocket ship in July 2021, it was a milestone for female astronauts. As a young aviator Ms Funk had excelled in her tests as part of the Women in Space programme. But despite the competence of the programme's participants, the scheme was cancelled in 1961. Ms Funk's voyage, at the age of 82, was the first time that any of the Mercury 13, as she and her colleagues became known, made it into space. She became the 67th woman to do so. But female astronauts are far outnumbered by men, and besides a legacy of sexism they face some unique problems. For instance, America's space agency, NASA, has rules that do not allow female astronauts to fly as much as their male counterparts. Where did this rule come from?

Earth's atmosphere is constantly being bombarded with charged particles, mainly from the Sun and galactic cosmic rays (heavy, high-energy ions stripped of their electrons and travelling close to the speed of light). Fortunately, Earth has a magnetic field that stretches to about 65,000km above its surface on the side facing the Sun, and much farther than that on the other side. This acts as a shield against the harmful rays. But beyond it astronauts are exposed to high levels of ionising radiation. This raises the risk of cancer, cardiovascular disease and cognitive impairment caused by damage to the nervous system.

Studying the effect of space radiation is hard. NASA has largely based its models on a study that periodically tracks survivors of the atomic bombs dropped on Japan during the second world war. This research found women to be at a higher risk of developing cancer than men when exposed to radiation, partly because they live longer, but also because they are more likely to suffer certain cancers, such as those of the breast and thyroid. To limit these dangers NASA imposes a career limit for radiation exposure, which is supposed to keep the chance of developing radiation-induced fatal cancer to 3% above that of non-astronauts. This means a 30-year-old woman would be limited to exposure equivalent to 180 millisieverts (mSv), whereas the limit for a 55-year-old man would be 400mSv. (On Earth, the average American is exposed to about 3mSv a year.) Astronauts taking a 180-day trip to the International Space Station face exposure of 50–120mSv. Peggy Whitson, a former chief of NASA's astronaut corps, has said that this ceiling means a female astronaut can fly only 45–50% of the number of missions that a male astronaut can.

NASA wants to replace this system with a standard career limit of 600mSv for all its astronauts, which would bring it into line with most other major space agencies. Raising the career limit for women, while reducing it for men, would give women a better chance of being selected for missions. But some men, particularly older astronauts, would lose out, particularly when it comes to decisions about who can go to the Moon, which is almost 400,000km away from Earth. The new rules could also pose problems as humans set their sights on Mars, which even at its closest to Earth is around 55 million km away. The researchers predict that a trip to the red planet would exceed the new radiation limit by 150%. They recommend individual risk assessments for each pilot based on their age and sex, and waivers for trips which would exceed the limits. Radiation risk should not have been an issue for Ms Funk, however. New Shepard made a suborbital flight to an altitude of 106km. That is beyond the Kármán line, which for many people defines the boundary of space, but is still safely inside Earth's magnetic field.

Why did Australia suffer from a plague of mice?

Australians share their country with some of the most fearsome predators on Earth, including the funnel-web spider, the inland taipan snake and the saltwater crocodile. But during 2021 it was a different beastie that caused havoc: the tiny house mouse. Their numbers exploded, resulting in one of the worst plagues of mice in decades, with the rodents particularly numerous in the south-east of the country. They ravaged crops, infested houses and even bit people in their beds. What caused Australia to be overrun with mice?

The blame could be laid at the feet of the British. Two centuries ago Australia was one of the last continental landmasses to be free of *Mus musculus*, the house mouse. When in 1788 the first fleet of British ships arrived in New South Wales to found a penal colony, both convicts and rodents were on board. The mice quickly spread, causing a headache for farmers trying to cultivate the land. Over the past century, outbreaks of mice have been occurring more frequently, hitting grain-growing regions of southern and eastern Australia hard. One of the worst recorded plagues caused A$64.5m ($43m) worth of damage in 1993, equivalent to A$84m today.

The weather was to blame for the latest outbreak. Studies show a tendency for plagues of mice to follow prolonged or severe droughts. One possible explanation is that once conditions improve, the short reproduction cycle of mice means their numbers can rebound much more quickly than those of their predators. After two years of drought and devastating bushfires from 2017 to 2019, heavy rains allowed grain growers to plant the largest area of winter crop ever recorded, with farmers sowing more than 23m hectares of land. The bumper harvest in 2020 created ideal conditions for a mass mouse-breeding season.

The result was one of the costliest plagues the country has ever seen, causing at least A$500m in damage to crops and grain stores. New South Wales sought the federal government's approval to use bromadiolone, a poison that is normally banned. Laced over large tracts of land by drone or tractor, it can wipe out the mice en masse. But critics argued that the poison could find its way into the food chain and harm other animals too, and regulators refused to approve its use. A combination of pesticides, heavy rain and flooding seemed to have subdued the plague by the end of 2021. But numbers did not collapse completely, and there were worrying signs in May 2022 that another outbreak was about to begin.

How many oceans are there, and who decides?

A new ocean has appeared on the maps of the National Geographic Society, an American research and conservation organisation. The Southern Ocean, which encircles Antarctica, will henceforth be given the same status, and typeface, as the Arctic, Atlantic, Indian and Pacific Oceans. Of course, the Southern Ocean is not really new. Not only has the body of water been there for around 30m years, ever since Antarctica and South America moved apart, but what to call it has been debated and contested by others before. So how many oceans are there – and who decides?

All Earth's oceans are part of one interconnected system. Mapmakers divide the waters into different zones with different names, including oceans, which also contain smaller seas. Oceans are usually bordered by whole continents, whereas seas are typically surrounded by smaller bits of land. But where two bodies of water converge, scientists must look at the conditions in the water to decide their boundaries. Bodies of water often have multiple names, which often reflect competing political claims. For instance, the water between Japan and the Koreas is known as the Sea of Japan in Japan, the East Sea in South Korea and the Korean East Sea in North Korea. Most governments have departments responsible for surveying, mapping and naming oceanographic features, but the global arbiter of such matters is the International Hydrographic Organisation (IHO), to which 94 countries belong.

The definition adopted by the National Geographic Society is that the Southern Ocean includes most of the waters that surround Antarctica to a latitude of 60° south, excluding the Drake Passage and Scotia Sea. Also called the "60th parallel south", this cartographic line roughly corresponds with the path of the Antarctic Circumpolar Current, which swirls water clockwise from west to east and marks a boundary between the cold, northward-flowing waters of the Antarctic and warmer sub-Antarctic waters. The waters of the Southern Ocean are colder and less saline than those of the southern Atlantic, Pacific and Indian Oceans, which has allowed a distinct ecosystem to flourish, rich in plant and animal life including krill, penguins, seals, whales and albatrosses. The United States Board on Geographic Names already counts the Southern Ocean as distinct from other oceans, also using the 60th-parallel definition. So do plenty of other governments, scientists and organisations.

But the IHO's position is trickier. The first edition of its marine mapping bible, *Limits of Oceans and Seas*, was published in 1928. This showed the Southern Ocean extending to Africa, Australia and South America. By the second edition, in 1937, the Southern Ocean's northern limits had been moved southward, so that they no longer touched land. In the third edition, in 1953, the Southern Ocean was omitted entirely as the IHO no longer saw a justification for applying the term ocean to this body of water, "the northern limits of which are difficult to lay down owing to their seasonal change". Instead the Atlantic, Indian and Pacific Oceans were all extended down to Antarctica.

Then in 2000, when the fourth edition of *Limits of Oceans and Seas* was due to be published, IHO members voted to name the waters below the 60th parallel south the "Southern Ocean". Argentina objected, as did Australia, which argues that it is the Southern Ocean, not the Indian Ocean, which laps its southern shores. But other disputes between members, such as what to call the Sea of Japan, stopped the fourth edition from being formally ratified. All of which leaves the IHO stuck in 1953, when the Southern Ocean did not exist at all. As a result there are one, four or five oceans, depending on who you ask. Best to take the answer with a pinch of salt.

Why suicide became rarer during the pandemic

In May 2020 the Australian Medical Association (AMA) issued a warning on mental health. Amid the outbreak of severe acute respiratory syndrome (SARS) in 2003, the suicide rate rose among elderly women in Hong Kong. Studies suggest that suicide is also more common during recessions. Based on these precedents, the AMA projected that covid-19 could cause a 25% increase in suicides. In some scenarios, the AMA warned, extra deaths from self-harm could exceed those caused by covid-19 itself.

Fortunately, this does not seem to have come to pass. Data from the Australian states of New South Wales, Queensland and Victoria show that there were 2% fewer suicides between April and September 2020 than in the same period in 2019. Australia had a mild pandemic relative to other Western countries, however. Yet even places that covid-19 ravaged show a similar pattern. A study of 21 countries in the *Lancet* measured how suicide rates changed between the first and second quarters of 2020, after adjusting for seasonality and for the long-run trend in each country before the pandemic began. In the median jurisdiction with available numbers – many data sources were sub-national, such as provinces – there were 10% fewer suicides between April and June 2020 than expected, and 7% fewer than in the same months of 2019. Weighted by population, the average declines were 7% relative to expectations and 11% compared with 2019.

The study focused on the early months of the pandemic. In theory, the problem could have grown worse over time. Suicides did surge in Japan in late 2020, yielding the country's first year-on-year rise since 2009. Its government appointed a "minister of loneliness" in response. But in the first quarter of 2021 Japan's suicide rate returned to its pre-pandemic level. Numbers from other countries do not show evidence of a spike in suicides either. The *Lancet* authors analysed the subset of jurisdictions for which data were available up to October 2020, and found similar trends to those from the second quarter of that year. Beyond that study,

Welcome reprieve

Number of suicides in April–July 2020 as % of those expected based on pre-covid-19 trends*

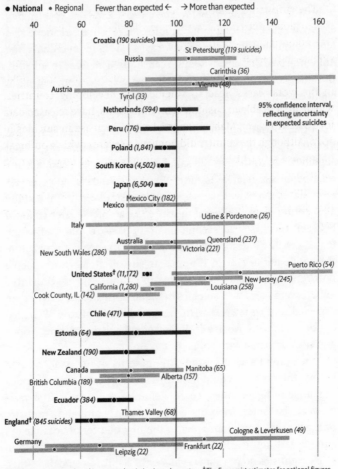

*Based on long-run trends and/or seasonal variation in each country   †*The Economist* estimates for national figures
Sources: "Suicide trends in the early months of the covid-19 pandemic", by J. Pirkis et al., *The Lancet Psychiatry*, 2021;
national statistics; *The Economist*

England reported a 12% decline in the year to September. And in America, a paper by scholars from the Centres for Disease Control and Prevention found a 6% drop in 2020.

The surprising stability of suicide rates suggests that broadly shared gloom does not necessarily predict deep individual despair. One potential explanation is that by providing fiscal support that shielded citizens from the financial consequences of the pandemic, governments in rich countries reduced a cause of stress that could, in the worst cases, lead to suicide. Few developing countries, which are less able to cushion economic blows, have released data for 2020. However, Malawi reported a 52% increase in suicides in 2020. Although the country did not have a severe covid-19 outbreak or impose strict lockdowns, its economy slowed down sharply. More data are needed from other countries with weak social-security safety nets to verify the hypothesis, but it seems likely that the financial lifelines offered by some governments kept many especially vulnerable people alive.

How do they do that? Good and bad deeds explained

How do you clean up an oil spill?

The *Safer*, a 45-year-old oil tanker, has been rusting off the west coast of Yemen since 2015. It lies 9km from the port of Hodeida, which is under the control of Houthi rebels. A stalwart crew of just seven people oversees the corroding ship and its cargo of almost 1.1m barrels of oil. A spill would disrupt the clean-water supply of around 9m people, according to a study published in October 2021 by researchers at Stanford University and the University of California, Berkeley. If the worst happens, how might it get cleaned up?

Nature does much of the work on its own. In the first 12 hours after a marine oil spill, as much as 50% of the lightest compounds turn into vapour and evaporate. The heavier gloop left behind is then weathered by waves, sunlight and oxygen, and is eventually broken down into smaller pieces that dissolve or drop to the seafloor. Micro-organisms also love munching on oil. But this biodegradation can take years. Because of this, human intervention is necessary. Clean-up efforts encourage bacteria to grow by adding nutrients such as phosphorus and nitrogen. But this process is still slow, requiring other methods to deal with what remains.

Floating barriers, called booms, are the first line of defence. They act as a wall above and below the water's surface, containing the oil and stopping it from reaching the shore. But booms are ineffective in choppy or icy waters. In a storm, waves can easily crash over them, tear them apart and wash them ashore. Another approach involves setting oil on the surface ablaze. Deciding whether to ignite an oil slick requires a trade-off: it will emit carbon dioxide and cause air pollution. But if left alone, the oil could spread over a larger area, causing damage more widely and making it harder to clean up. Skimming devices are a more high-tech option. The tools are designed to separate oil from water and release the clean water back into the sea. But they tend to suck up more water than oil. In 2010, when the *Deepwater Horizon* disaster caused an oil leak into the Gulf of Mexico, officials called in *A Whale*, a Taiwanese-owned super-skimmer ship. It could supposedly collect up to 21m gallons (95m litres) of contaminated water per day, but it sucked up virtually no oil during two weeks of tests.

The ship's owners blamed this less-than-slick performance on large quantities of chemical dispersants poured into the water. These are the fourth method of dealing with a spill. They break down the oil into smaller droplets that easily mix with water. But they too are an imperfect solution. Not only do they make other clean-up methods such as skimming harder, but they may be even more damaging to the environment than oil. Studies have found that Corexit, the chemical dispersant used in the *Deepwater Horizon* spill, was 50 times more toxic to corals in the Gulf of Mexico than oil was on its own. And thousands of clean-up workers who were exposed to it suffered health problems, including coughing, skin irritation and burning in the eyes, nose, throat or lungs. Several countries, including Britain and Sweden, have banned it.

Once lots of oil seeps into water, it is all but impossible to remove it effectively. The proportion that is recovered is often just 10–15%, according to the International Tanker Owners Pollution Federation, a shipping-industry body. Just 21% of the oil released by *Deepwater Horizon* was either burned or chemically dispersed (a further 17% was pumped up through broken pipes). That is slightly better than the *Exxon Valdez* spill in 1989, in which about 14% of the oil was recovered. Researchers and start-ups are, however, picking up the slack. Vinayak Dravid and Vikas Nandwana, of Northwestern University in Illinois, have developed a reusable carbon-based sponge capable of absorbing more than 30 times its weight in oil. A soap composed of iron-rich salts, created by researchers at the University of Bristol, also has potential. It can magnetise the oil droplets dispersed in water, making them easier to retrieve. Robots such as Seaswarm, developed by scientists at the Massachusetts Institute of Technology, and microscopic submarines could also one day help do the job.

But the prospect of a spill from the *Safer*, even with new technologies in the works, is grim. In March 2022 Houthi rebels agreed to a UN proposal to offload the oil. But when this will happen is unclear. Yemen's war has turned the country into one of the most wretched places on Earth. Pouring oil on troubled waters, in this case, risks making things much worse.

How do you fight a wildfire?

Wildfires can be sparked by lightning, though more often they have a human cause, such as downed power lines, carelessly discarded cigarettes, campfires or arson. The first sign is usually smoke, spotted by a member of the public or via cameras set up in high-risk, remote areas. The tactics used to fight wildfires are much the same the world over, and have changed little in recent decades. Response teams in land vehicles, planes or helicopters are mobilised to use water and fire-retardant chemicals to try to dampen the flames. Crews of firefighters also create "fire lines" that the conflagration cannot cross, by removing vegetation and digging down to the dirt. It can be expensive, resource-intensive work.

Once they reach a certain size, however, fires simply release too much energy to be fought, explains Alexander Held, a fire ecologist at the European Forest Institute. Water evaporates before it reaches the flames and it becomes impossible to get near enough to contain the blaze. In these cases, there is often little to do but wait for changes in weather, wind or topography that might make the fire controllable once more.

Fire crews are busier than ever, yet their toolkit no longer seems sufficient. Although the proportion of fires that become large and difficult to contain each year (2–3% in America) is not increasing, those that do get big are doing more damage. Six of the 20 largest blazes ever seen in California ignited in 2020, which was the worst year for wildfires in the state's history, according to the National Interagency Fire Centre. And the damage they cause is getting worse as more people live in the areas next to forests. Climate change is adding to the woe, as temperatures rise and droughts become more severe in places already prone to burning. The American West is becoming more arid. Hot and dry conditions turn grassland and forest into kindling.

The policy of fire suppression, introduced in the 20th century, is increasingly being questioned. Trying to put out every fire results in greater stores of unburned fuel – including dried grass, shrub, trees, leaves and forest matter – to feed subsequent fires. In earlier times indigenous and agricultural societies started fires deliberately, or allowed smaller wildfires to burn. This got rid of fuel and reduced the risk of a larger, uncontrollable fire later on. Such practices were mostly abandoned after technology created the illusion that all conflagrations could, and should, be extinguished. But experts are now advocating a shift from suppressing to managing fires through better land management. This includes making sure that landscapes include breaks that fires cannot cross. In 2017 four large wildfires killed 65 people in Portugal, the deadliest in its history. The country subsequently decided to prioritise land management, including the creation of buffer zones and the setting of deliberate fires during the winter, when they can be controlled. Portugal has not suffered a disastrous blaze since.

Starting controlled fires or selectively letting small wildfires burn might be the right strategy, but it can be a hard sell. The public sees fires as dangerous and expects firefighters to put them out if they possibly can. Few decision-makers are specialists in wildfires, and the priorities of firefighting forces and those who control land are not necessarily aligned. Better understanding of wildfires' behaviour would help those on the ground decide which can be left alone. Buildings in fire-prone areas can be designed to be more resilient. But work also needs to be done to change public perceptions. To cope with fires, humans must relearn how to live with them.

How can you maximise your chances of winning a Nobel prize?

The Nobel prizes, awarded each year in the fields of physics, chemistry, physiology or medicine, literature and peace, may be the world's most coveted awards. As soon as a new crop of laureates is named, critics start comparing the victors' achievements with those of previous winners, reigniting debates over past snubs. Stephen Hawking, for example, was never awarded the physics prize for his work on black holes, and never can be, having died in 2018 (the prizes are never awarded posthumously). A full account of why not will have to wait until 2068: the Nobel Foundation's rules prevent disclosure about the selection process for 50 years. But once this statute of limitations ends, the foundation reveals who offered nominations, and whom they endorsed. Its data start in 1901 and end in 1953 for medicine; 1966 for physics, chemistry and literature; and 1967 for peace.

Nomination lists do not explain omissions like Leo Tolstoy (who got 19 nominations) or Mahatma Gandhi (who got 12). But they do show that between 1901 and 1966, Nobel voters handed out awards more in the style of a private members' club than a survey of expert opinion. Whereas candidates with lots of nominations often fell short, those with the right backers – such as Albert Einstein or other laureates – fared better. This suggests that the way to maximise your chances of winning a Nobel is to be nominated by a previous winner.

The bar to a Nobel nomination is low. For the peace prize, public officials, jurists and the like submit names to a committee, chosen by Norway's parliament, that picks the winner. For the others, Swedish academies solicit names from thousands of people, mostly professors, and hold a vote for the laureate. On average, 55 nominations per year were filed for each prize in between 1901 and 1966. Historically, voters paid little heed to consensus among nominators. In literature and medicine, the candidate with the most nominations won just 11% and 12% of the time; in peace

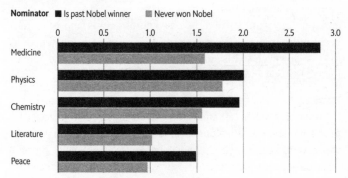

For whom Nobel tolls
Post-nomination win ratio,* 1901–66

Nombinator ■ Is past Nobel winner ■ Never won Nobel

*Ratio of prizes won anytime after a nomination to the number expected
if all nominators had equal influence, in year of nomination
Source: Nobel Foundation

and chemistry, the rates were 23% and 26%. Only in physics, at
42%, did the most nominated candidates have a big advantage. In
1956 Ramón Menéndez Pidal, a linguist and historian, got 60% of
nominations for the literature prize, but still lost.

However, voters did make one group of nominators happy:
current and future laureates. Candidates put forward by past victors
went on to win at some point in the future 40% more often than
did those whose nominators never won a Nobel themselves. People
whose nominators later became laureates also won unusually often.
This implies that being accomplished enough to merit future Nobel
consideration was sufficient to gain extra influence over voters. In
theory, this imbalance could simply reflect laureates nominating
stronger candidates. However, at least one Nobel winner seems to
have boosted his nominees' chances, rather than merely naming
superstars who would have won anyway.

According to the Nobel Foundation's online archive, all 11 of
Einstein's nominees won a prize. Some were already famous, such
as Max Planck; others, such as Walther Bothe, were lesser known.
In two cases, Einstein's support seems to have been decisive. In

1940 Einstein supported Otto Stern, a physicist who already had 60 nominations. Stern won the next time the prize was given. Similarly, Wolfgang Pauli, whose exclusion principle is central to quantum mechanics, had received 20 nominations before Einstein backed him in 1945. He got his prize that same year. Einstein died in 1955, however, so his sure-fire backing is no longer available to today's Nobel wannabes.

How do you make synthetic diamonds?

Despite Shirley Bassey's refrain, belted out at the start of a James Bond film from 1971, diamonds may not be for ever – at least when it comes to natural ones. In May 2021 Pandora became the first big jeweller to announce that it will no longer sell mined diamonds. Instead it will use gems made in a laboratory. Even mining companies are getting in on the act. In 2018 De Beers, the world's largest miner of diamonds by value, launched a brand called Lightbox to sell jewellery featuring the synthetic stones. But how are these gemstones different from those found underground – and how can diamonds be replicated in a lab?

Natural diamonds were formed more than 1bn years ago deep below cratons, the oldest parts of continents. There, between the planet's core and its crust, the pressure and temperature were just right to crystallise carbon into its hardest form. Diamonds would have remained there were it not for molten rock rushing through the mantle, drawing them up towards the Earth's surface. This provided the deposits that firms such as De Beers mine today. But in the 1950s General Electric, an American industrial conglomerate, developed a process to make diamonds by artificially crystallising carbon under 10 gigapascals of pressure – equivalent to the weight of 64 elephants placed on the point of a ballet dancer's shoe – and temperatures above 2,000°C. This process was enormously expensive and energy-intensive. And until recently the stones produced were too unrefined, too uniform in colour and sometimes too unattractively yellow (because of excess nitrogen in their chemistry) to make attractive jewellery. For a long time the main uses for lab-grown diamonds were industrial, where they are valued for their strength, for instance as the tips of heavy-duty drills.

But scientists have since developed processes that can create synthetic diamonds at a fraction of the cost and time it took in the 1950s – and they look more like the real thing, too. Pandora's new collection of lab-grown diamond jewellery will be produced using chemical-vapour deposition (CVD), a technique commonly used in the production of semiconductors. In a plasma reactor as hot as the sun, atomised gases produce carbon atoms that attach to the crystal lattice of a natural-diamond seed, known as a substrate, forming a new diamond good enough to set in a ring. On average it costs $300–500 per carat (one carat is equivalent to 0.2g) to produce a diamond by CVD, according to a report in 2018 by Bain, a consultancy. That is a tenth of the price from a decade earlier. And synthetic diamonds are offered to shoppers at about a third of the price of a mined stone.

Jewellers hope that lab-grown wares will help revive flagging sales of diamonds. Production of real diamonds fell by more than a quarter between 2017 and 2020 to 111m carats, according to Bain. Demand has been hit in part because of worries about ethical sourcing. *Blood Diamond*, a film from 2006 starring Leonardo DiCaprio, highlighted how the diamond trade helps fund criminal and rebel groups in Africa. Lab-grown diamonds provide a morally acceptable – and cheaper – alternative. Even so, until synthetic diamonds become truly cheap, there are fewer noble reasons to avoid buying a pricey ring. Given the recessions caused by the covid-19 pandemic, newly engaged couples may prefer to spend their money on something less frivolous than a rock, no matter how it was produced.

How do you transport a horse from one country to another?

Prestigious equestrian events and horse races are an international industry. Events such as CHIO Aachen, in Germany, and the Kentucky Derby, in America, attract riders and their mounts from across the world. For the equestrian events at the 2021 Olympic and Paralympic games, 325 horses from 50 countries travelled to Tokyo. How do horses get to these competitions?

Horses' owners have always taken advantage of the latest technologies. Steeds have been transported by sea since ancient times. By the 19th century some racing horses were being moved around in vans, first pulled by other horses, later by motor vehicles. In 1912 horses travelled across Europe by rail and road for the Olympic games in Stockholm, which was the first to include the sort of equestrian events seen today. These days, horses travel by aeroplane. After being coaxed into air-conditioned stables, called pallets, they are loaded onto specially configured planes. In flight, grooms provide them with special water-enhanced hay to keep them hydrated. (They also pack tonnes of baggage, including saddles, shoes and pitchforks.) Pilots who know they have horses on board try to take off and land more gradually to keep their equine passengers steady.

Preparing for travel can take months. The animals must have vaccinations, export licences and passports detailing their size and identifying marks. Biosecurity is taken seriously. An outbreak of equine herpes virus in Europe in 2021 prompted the sport's governing body, the International Federation for Equestrian Sports, to introduce new health measures. Much like their owners, horses had to have their temperatures checked and take a polymerase-chain-reaction (PCR) test before travel – but for equine herpes, not covid-19. Only then could they begin their pre-travel quarantine.

Most countries require some period of isolation before a flight, although its length depends on where the animals have travelled from. For the Tokyo Olympics, horses from around the world were sent to Europe for 60 days of health surveillance followed by seven days of strict quarantine. They were then flown on 19 Emirates cargo flights from Liege, in Belgium, to Tokyo, via Dubai. (Liege is home to Peden Bloodstock, the world's largest firm of horse-shipping agents, so it has become a hub for equine transport.) On arrival at Haneda airport in Tokyo the animals were taken by lorry to a purpose-built equestrian Olympic village at Baji Koen, which was also a quarantine bubble, for the duration of the competition.

Horses are better at flying than humans. They can sleep comfortably while upright and they rehydrate quickly. They seem to deal well with jet lag too. But moving them is an expensive business. A return flight for one horse and its kit from America to Europe can cost $25,000 in "business class" (two to a pallet), which owners prefer, although a cheaper "economy" (three sharing) ticket might be available. Prices rose during the pandemic. Owners of course have no guarantee that they will recoup their costs in prize money and (later) stud fees. But sometimes they do. Black Caviar, who was mostly ridden by Luke Nolen, an Australian jockey, regularly flew first class (alone in a pallet) from Melbourne to London in order to race at Ascot. That cost around $50,000 per trip. But given that she made more than $7m in prizes over the course of her racing career, the equine air fares paid off.

How can cities prepare for flooding?

In September 2021 stormwater gushed into subway stations in New York City and turned streets into bubbling rivers. Across America's north-east, flash floods caused by extreme rain from the remnants of Hurricane Ida killed more than 50 people. In July that year similar scenes played out in Zhengzhou, a city in China, where nearly 300 people were killed in a deluge. Flooding caused by storm surges and tropical storms has long been a risk for cities close to sea level such as Miami or Amsterdam. But by changing precipitation patterns and increasing the amount of water that clouds hold, a warming atmosphere means that storms are now dumping more water onto cities. How can they learn to cope?

Urban environments are not well suited to extreme rainfall because concrete stops water draining away. Accordingly, one of the best things cities can do is to become more porous. By 2030 China wants to cover 30 cities with sponge-like features, which promise to soak up or re-use 80% of rainfall, at an estimated cost of $1trn. These include "permeable pavements", which allow water to move through them, and "green roofs", which use plants and soil to collect and filter rainwater. Lower-tech solutions can help too. Planting trees and shrubs along streets can reduce run-off. One study in British Columbia found that urban trees can intercept roughly half the rainfall. Cities can also stop water flowing where it shouldn't. In Rotterdam, the second-largest city in the Netherlands, playgrounds, sports facilities and parks are built to make space for water. And simply tidying up makes a difference too. Rubbish left out on the streets for collection, as it is in many American cities, blocks water from flowing into drains.

Many of the worst problems occur below street level. Sewers often struggle to cope, regurgitating their contents back up into homes, streets and waterways. London is building a new "super sewer", due to be completed by 2025, partly to avoid this. Greater Chicago, which is in essence built on a swamp, has since the mid-1970s been building the "Deep Tunnel", designed to divert sewage and storm water into holding reservoirs. But though much of the system is operational, it continues to be overwhelmed during extreme storms, forcing the city to dump effluent into Lake Michigan. Flash floods can also play havoc with underground transport systems. At least 14 people died in the city of Zhengzhou in China after rising water trapped commuters in tunnels. Such tragedies can be avoided. In Taipei subway entrances have been elevated to stop water coming in during typhoons. Tokyo's metro system is equipped with sliding doors capable of withstanding floodwater. And at least 11 people who died in New York as a result of the flooding in 2021 were in basement apartments, many of which are illegal and lack safety measures such as multiple exits. The city's latest flood plan – released in May 2021 – outlined a scheme to notify people living in basements of flood risks but did not intend to start doing so until 2023.

In many cases, officials and residents fail to treat flood risks with the gravity they deserve. For example, the European Flood Awareness System, an early warning system developed by the European Commission, sent out specific warnings to German officials four days before a violent downpour began in July 2021. Despite that, many residents in the worst-affected regions were caught off guard, and more than 180 people died in Germany. And in Zhengzhou, a forecast of heavy rains from meteorologists that month was largely ignored by the city's authorities, and its 10m inhabitants were warned too late. Days later more than 300,000 residents of Ningbo, another Chinese city, were relocated after the first warnings of a typhoon. Despite widespread flooding, no deaths were reported. Like many consequences of climate change, heavier and more sudden rainfall is something that cities must adapt to. But sometimes it is so severe that the only thing to do is get people out of the way.

How will the next Dalai Lama be chosen?

The Dalai Lama turned 86 in July 2021. By all accounts he is in good health, but questions about his successor become more complicated with each birthday. Tenzin Gyatso, the 14th Dalai Lama, is the highest spiritual figure in Tibetan Buddhism and the founder of the Tibetan government-in-exile, based in Dharamsala in northern India. His incumbency has encompassed a period of rule in Tibet by the Chinese Communist Party (CCP), which annexed Tibet in 1951. For decades the Dalai Lama has been a thorn in the side of the CCP. Tibetan Buddhists believe that the next Dalai Lama will be reincarnated and identified by a council of senior disciples. The Chinese government insists it has the right to anoint his successor. America and India have also entered the fray. How will the next Dalai Lama be chosen?

In Tibetan Buddhism, each Dalai Lama is a *tulku*, a reincarnated custodian of the teachings of Avalokiteśvara, the bodhisattva (enlightened being) of compassion. When a Dalai Lama dies, it normally takes years to identify his reincarnated form. Tenzin Gyatso was identified in 1937, four years after the 13th Dalai Lama died. Senior monks interpreted signs from the 13th's death, such as an unusual star-shaped fungus that grew on his shrine apparently pointing to the north-east, to direct their search. Various clues and spiritual masters led them to two-year-old Tenzin Gyatso, then known as Lhamo Dhondup, who was the right age to be the reincarnated *tulku*. Young Tenzin correctly identified items belonging to the deceased Dalai Lama and on February 22nd 1940 was enthroned as the 14th Dalai Lama.

According to Chinese law the central government must approve the next Dalai Lama or any other senior living Buddha. The atheist regime has long weighed in on matters of spiritual succession. On May 14th 1995, a six-year-old called Gedhun Choekyi Nyima was declared by the Dalai Lama to be the 11th Panchen Lama, the second-most-senior monk in Tibetan Buddhism. Three days later he disappeared; he has not been seen in public since. The Chinese government named its own Panchen Lama, who is rejected by most Tibetans. The Dalai Lama has condemned Chinese efforts to appoint his successor as "brazen meddling". He has even raised the possibility that he may be the last Dalai Lama.

But the dispute is not just between China and the Tibetans. Another option floated by the Dalai Lama is that his reincarnation may be identified outside Tibet, perhaps in India, where he fled to in 1959 after a failed Tibetan uprising against Chinese rule. An Indian *tulku* would inflame an already tense relationship between India and China. In May 2020 a skirmish broke out on the disputed border between China and India (Tibet sits on the Chinese side). That India hosts the Tibetan government-in-exile is a "security buffer" as well as a "soft-power resource", says Dibyesh Anand of the University of Westminster. This is particularly apparent in disputed territories such as Arunachal Pradesh in north-east India, which is inhabited by many Tibetan Buddhists. A Chinese-anointed Dalai Lama could be "weaponised by China" to lay claim to the region, notes Mr Anand. In April 2021 Bloomberg reported that senior government officials in Delhi were discussing how to influence the choice of the next Dalai Lama. America has also weighed in: in December 2021 Congress passed the Tibet Policy and Support Act. It states that only Tibetans can choose the next Dalai Lama and that Chinese officials who interfere will be subject to sanctions.

The Dalai Lama is aware of these tensions. He says that when he is about 90 he will consult other high lamas for advice. The irony is that despite being called a "splittist" by the CCP, the Dalai Lama advocates only Tibetan autonomy within China, and has acted as a moderating force against those calling for full independence and perhaps a violent uprising. If the Chinese government meddles with the reincarnation process, it will only strengthen those who want full independence for Tibet. That would be even more worrying for Chinese rulers than a Dalai Lama they cannot control.

How do people and companies avoid paying taxes?

A mega-leak of documents to the International Consortium of Investigative Journalists (ICIJ) made a splash in October 2021 when media around the world began running stories on what they have dubbed the Pandora Papers. The exposé lifted the lid on the financial affairs of dozens of world leaders, other public officials and billionaires in 91 countries. The focus of this leak, as with the ICIJ's past leaks, such as the Panama Papers in 2016 and the Paradise Papers a year later, was the offshore dealings of the global elite. The use of an offshore company to move money or buy property is not necessarily dodgy; a billionaire may mask a purchase made with legitimate wealth for privacy reasons. But shell companies registered in palm-fringed offshore centres (the British Virgin Islands is a favourite) are often used to avoid or evade tax, or to launder ill-gotten gains.

Individuals have various ways to avoid tax legally by using structured tax shelters or changing their place of residence. Tax evasion (rather than avoidance) is a different matter and is treated as a criminal offence in many countries (though Switzerland is famously more lenient). The smartest evaders use a combination of bank accounts, shell companies, trusts and foundations – often fronted by nominees – in one or more offshore financial centres. Corporate tax avoidance is a greyer legal area. Companies naturally push the envelope, often betting that the authorities will have neither the wit nor the resources to confront them over their tax-minimisation strategies – or that governments will accept less tax in return for investment by "mobile capital".

Denis Healey, a former British chancellor of the exchequer, once described the difference between tax evasion and avoidance as "the thickness of a prison wall". Both grew in line with financial globalisation in the late 20th century. Evasion became easier with the explosion of tax havens, which was tacitly endorsed by rich countries (especially Britain) that saw them as useful adjuncts to their own financial centres. Today the world has as many as 50 tax havens, some of them more accurately described as "secrecy jurisdictions". Not all are offshore: American states such as South Dakota and Nevada peddle secrecy through the trusts they offer. Multinationals, meanwhile, have found ingenious ways to exploit loopholes in cross-border tax rules, which were designed for an earlier age. International and bilateral tax agreements that were designed to avoid double taxation can be gamed to produce double non-taxation.

The pushback against such ruses began in the late 1990s, when the Organisation for Economic Co-operation and Development (OECD), a rich-country forum, declared war on "harmful tax competition". It has waxed and waned since then, reaching a new level of intensity since 2008 as cash-strapped countries, both rich and poor, have fought harder to claw back lost tax revenues. Tax havens have, under intense pressure, agreed to exchange more information on clients with their home countries. The world is moving towards a system of automatic exchange of data, even as some countries grumble that this clashes with their privacy laws. Others complain that they are being bullied into providing data without a guarantee of reciprocation from America and other large economies. Still, life has become a lot harder over the past few years for individuals looking to dodge their tax obligations, and is likely to get tougher still.

Reform of the international rules for companies has proved trickier, but some 140 countries and territories, including all the big economies, struck a deal in October 2021 that aims to align taxation more closely with where sales are made, and introduce a minimum global tax rate of 15%. However, it is too much to expect the closure of all the loopholes, and new ones are sure to open up. Rich-world governments have long tacitly encouraged certain types of avoidance for fear of otherwise being branded uncompetitive and turning off big investors. They may be less keen on billionaires dodging tax in personal property deals, but also reluctant to target plutocrats who make generous political donations. The Pandora Papers won't be the last in the series.

How do repressive regimes use internet shutdowns?

On September 26th 2021 residents of the state of Rajasthan in northwest India discovered that their mobile phones could no longer connect to the internet. For several hours services such as WhatsApp, Facebook and Google Maps were rendered useless. The outage was no accident. District officials explained they had ordered internet providers to shut off access to pre-empt cheating in an exam for highly coveted teacher positions in the state's school system. But the shutdown affected millions more. In Jaipur, Rajasthan's capital, an estimated 80,000 shops and businesses were forced to close.

This was not the first time India's government has pulled the plug on its citizens. Access Now, a New York-based advocacy group, reckons that state and local authorities in the country have shut down mobile-phone or broadband networks about 500 times since 2016. And although India is the worst offender, it is not the only one. According to Access Now, 66 countries have implemented shutdowns, in some form or another, since 2016 (see map overleaf). In 2019 alone there were 213 such incidents.

Shutdowns have become more sophisticated in recent years. Authorities have learned to block specific platforms, such as WhatsApp or Twitter, to discourage political mobilisation. They may also ask internet services providers to throttle, or deliberately slow down, network traffic or limit only mobile-internet connections. Shutdowns may affect individual cities or entire countries; they may last a few hours or drag on for months. When a civil war broke out in Ethiopia's Tigray region in November 2020, access was shut off within hours, and had still not been restored at the time of writing, 16 months later.

The motivations for such interruptions are usually political. India has ordered internet shutdowns to quell local protests and to stamp out civil unrest, especially in the Kashmir valley. In 2021 Uganda, Niger and the Democratic Republic of Congo imposed blackouts in the run-up to closely fought elections. Authorities

Dark web
Internet shutdowns, 2016–21*

0 1 2 5 10 25 50 500

Source: Access Now

*To May 2021

usually justify their actions on the grounds that they protect the public from hate speech or misinformation, but advocacy groups argue they suppress free speech and help to cover up human-rights abuses.

They are costly too. A study by the Brookings Institution, a Washington think-tank, found that internet shutdowns cost countries $2.4bn in lost GDP in 2016. Some consider them human-rights violations. In 2016 the United Nations passed a resolution declaring access to the internet to be a human right, and condemning "measures to intentionally prevent or disrupt access to our dissemination of information online". The resolution was passed without a vote but a number of countries supported amendments to weaken it. Among them were China, Russia and India.

Diplomatic niceties: oddities of international relations

Who controls the Arctic?

The Arctic Circle stretches roughly 9,900 miles (16,000km) around the Earth. It is the line north of which there is at least one day each year of total darkness and one day of total light. Eight countries have territory within it: America (through Alaska), Canada, Denmark (by virtue of Greenland), Finland, Iceland, Norway, Russia and Sweden. These eight make up the Arctic Council, a scientific-policy club, alongside 13 observer countries, including China, which calls itself a "near-Arctic state" and has plans for a "polar silk road" to make use of Arctic shipping routes and resource-extraction projects. Some of these states have jostled for control in the region.

Sergei Lavrov, Russia's foreign minister, claimed in May 2021 that his country controls the Arctic. "It has been absolutely clear for everyone for a long time that this is our territory," he said. Russian land makes up 53% of the Arctic coastline. Russia has also ramped up its military investment in the region: since 2007 at least 50 Soviet-era military outposts have reopened. But the other Arctic states see things differently. In 2018 NATO sent an aircraft carrier into the Arctic Circle for the first time in 27 years. In 2020 British and American warships entered the Barents Sea, north of Norway and close to Russia's key naval bases, for the first time since the 1980s. In early 2022 Norway carried out its biggest military exercise inside the Arctic Circle since the cold war. What explains this sabre-rattling, and who really controls the Arctic?

Most of the Arctic is ice or water. Increasingly it is the latter: in 2020 ice cover fell close to the lowest on record, with minimum cover almost 1m square miles smaller than the average minimum between 1981 and 2010. "Countries' interest in this region came about because of climate change," says Andreas Osthagen, of the Fridtjof Nansen Institute, near Oslo. Melting ice has opened a shipping corridor from the Bering Strait, between Siberia and Alaska, to the Barents Sea. The route remains frozen for up to nine months each year. But in 2020 more than 1,000 cargo ships made the trip – 25% more than the previous year. Russia controls the route, which runs through its territorial waters, and charges a fee for passage. But the opening up of the Northern Sea Route is a double-edged sword for Russia. Ice was the bastion that protected its northern coast; its disappearance makes the country more vulnerable. Ahead of a summit in Brussels in June 2021, NATO said that melting ice "could lead to new geopolitical tensions".

Arctic states are also competing to control the seabed: melting ice has made mineral deposits and oil and gas fields more accessible. To stake a claim beyond their territorial waters, which stretches 12 nautical miles from shore, countries must prove that the seabed is an extension of their continental shelf – part of the same landmass as their territory. The geology is subjective: Canada, Denmark and Russia all claim the Lomonosov Ridge, an underwater mountain range that runs beneath the North Pole. Some countries have gone to extremes to prove their point. In 2007 a Russian submarine planted a titanium tricolour flag on the seabed beneath the pole. In 2013 Canada issued a passport to Father Christmas. Such gestures might seem light-hearted, but alongside the increased military activity they constitute a real effort by governments to stake their claims. For now, Russia has the uppermost hand. But as the ice shrinks, other countries' interest in the Arctic will only grow.

Who governs a country's airspace?

When the crew of Ryanair flight FR4978 were told by Belarusian air-traffic controllers on May 23rd 2021 to divert to Minsk, ostensibly because of a bomb threat, the plane was actually closer to its intended destination, Vilnius, than to Minsk. But it was in Belarusian airspace. The true purpose of the diversion was to arrest Roman Protasevich, a journalistic thorn in the side of the regime of Alexander Lukashenko, Belarus's dictator. The characterisation by Ryanair's chief executive, Michael O'Leary, of the Belarusian antics as "state-sponsored piracy" seems accurate. But did international law compel his crew to land in Minsk (even without the fighter jet sent to encourage compliance)? Who governs a country's airspace? And what laws protect an airline's right to fly over a foreign country?

For the answers, go back to the treaties that set up the international trading system after the second world war. Aviation and shipping were excluded – the first because post-war Britain thought that competition from American airlines on routes to its colonies would drive London-based ones out of business. The resulting Chicago Convention of 1944 – which set up the International Civil Aviation Organisation (ICAO), which would become the United Nations' body for air transport – gave countries "complete and exclusive sovereignty" over the skies above their territories. Without an explicit agreement, airlines running scheduled passenger services, as Ryanair does, have no right to fly over foreign territory. Another treaty signed at the Chicago Convention, the International Air Services Transit Agreement, gave airlines registered in member countries these rights, but Belarus is not a signatory.

Belarus has bilateral agreements with other European countries to allow their airlines to use its airspace and its airports. It may have broken those it has with Poland (where the Ryanair plane was registered) or Ireland (where the airline's owner is headquartered). Mr Lukashenko's henchmen may have also run roughshod over other treaties. Although planes in flight are legally obliged to follow the instructions of air-traffic controllers, the Chicago Convention bans any use of civil aviation that may endanger safety; forcing a plane to divert and land under false pretences could come under that prohibition. An amendment to the convention in 1984 also forbids the use of "weapons against civil aircraft in flight".

There are also questions about whether the convention's "rules of the air" were broken by forcing the aircraft to divert to Minsk rather than Vilnius, a nearer and more suitable airport – if there really were explosives on board. Interception by a military jet should be a "last resort", and it is hard to see how that was true in this case, says Charles Stotler of the Centre for Air and Space Law at the University of Mississippi. Belarus is also party to treaties, originally signed in the early 1970s by nearly all UN members, that forbid communicating "information [known] to be false" that threatens aircraft safety, as well as the seizure of civil aircraft during a flight.

The International Air Transport Association, an airline lobby group, called for a full investigation. In January 2022 a UN report concluded that the bomb threat was indeed false. The problem is that there are few teeth with which to bite Belarus. ICAO was never meant to be a regulatory body, and can do little to punish errant member states beyond suspending their voting power. If Belarus has broken bilateral agreements with Poland or Ireland, neither country has the clout to take any meaningful action on its own. The treaties from the 1970s do not help either: they expect signatories to police themselves. Had aviation been included in post-war international trade treaties, breaches would be subject to the World Trade Organisation's dispute-settlement mechanism. (WTO members have in the past discussed including the sector.) But the mechanism is slow, and in any case intended to deal with quarrels about international commerce – not acts of piracy.

Who gets to be in the G7?

In the beginning there were six. The instigators were President Valéry Giscard d'Estaing of France and Chancellor Helmut Schmidt of Germany. In 1975 they were joined by the leaders of four other big Western industrialised countries – America, Britain, Italy and Japan – at the Château de Rambouillet near Paris to discuss the world economy, at the time beset by unemployment, inflation and energy woes. The addition of Canada the following year made it a Group of Seven (G7). A lot has changed in the decades since then, but one question has been persistent: who gets to be a member of the exclusive club?

Confusingly, group photographs at its summits show nine leaders rather than seven, because the presidents of the European Commission and the European Council also take part. Members are supposed to have two things in common: large economies and democratic values. That leaves plenty of room for debate about who should be included. When its GDP was reckoned to be edging above Canada's, some argued that Spain deserved a place at the top table, but a decision to let a country in has to be unanimous, and leaders like to keep the club cosy. In 1998 it did expand into a G8, with the addition of Russia, which seemed to be on a path to democracy – only to shrink back to seven again after Russia annexed Crimea in 2014. Compactness is no guarantee of cohesion, however. A divisive summit in 2018, after which President Donald Trump insulted his Canadian host, Justin Trudeau, and refused to sign the final communiqué, prompted talk of a "G6+1".

Mr Trump also complained that the membership of the club was "very outdated". He is right. Back in 1975 those few countries produced 70% of global GDP; their share has since shrunk to some 40%. After the global financial crisis of 2007–09 the broader G20, which includes big emerging markets such as Brazil, China and India, seemed more relevant and representative. Leaders holding the G7's annual rotating presidency have sought to compensate for the group's diminished heft by inviting important guests. Emmanuel

Macron, France's president, welcomed many African leaders, among others, to his summit in Biarritz in 2019. In Cornwall in 2021 Boris Johnson hosted the leaders of three Asia-Pacific democracies, Australia, India and South Korea. He proposed turning the G7 into the D10 ("D" stands for democracy).

That may hint at a future for the club. Shared values in the face of a growing challenge from Russia, China and other authoritarian countries could give it a renewed sense of purpose. It helps that in Joe Biden America once again has a president who believes in those values and in the power of alliances. The club still has the potential to set the global agenda – for example, pushing for a minimum global corporate-tax rate. And in February 2022 the G7 issued a condemnation of Russia's invasion of Ukraine, and imposed sanctions to isolate Russia's economy. Having left the European Union, Britain in particular is keen to revitalise the G7 as a global forum. But other G7 members worried that turning it into the D10 would make it seem too much of an anti-China club. Well into middle age and after a few health scares, the G7 cannot take its vigour for granted.

The beastly history of diplomatic insults

When Liz Truss, Britain's foreign secretary, flew to Moscow in February 2022 for talks with her Russian counterpart, Sergei Lavrov, she must have hoped her intervention would help to ease tensions over Ukraine. Things did not go to plan. At a press conference after the talks, Mr Lavrov compared the experience to a conversation of "the mute with the deaf", before walking off and leaving Ms Truss facing the cameras alone. Mr Lavrov is not known for his tact: in 2015 a microphone caught him referring to Saudi Arabian officials as "morons". And he is not the first to use insults as a tool of diplomacy. The history of world leaders exchanging verbal barbs is a long and catty one.

In the Ottoman empire, actions spoke louder than words. When Selim the Grim, the sultan from 1512 to 1520, wanted to announce his victory over Dulkadir, a buffer state between his empire and the Mamluk sultanate of Egypt, he sent an envoy to Cairo. When the ambassador was received, he opened a bag and hurled at the Mamluk sultan's feet the severed head of Dulkadir's ruler, one of the sultan's closest allies. Things did not get much friendlier; the Ottomans eventually invaded and conquered Egypt. In another grim escalation, in 1827, the governor of Algiers rashly flicked the French ambassador with a fly whisk and provoked more than 130 years of colonisation.

Modern diplomacy tends to be less physical, but just as fraught. Autocrats, perhaps unsurprisingly, show most disdain for their democratically elected opposite numbers. Hugo Chávez, Venezuela's president for 14 years from 1999, was known for his tirades against George W. Bush. He regularly referred to the American president as the devil, most famously at the United Nations General Assembly, when he spat, "It still smells of sulphur." Chávez had a well-thumbed thesaurus of taunts. In a televised speech in 2006 he said of Mr Bush, "You are an ignoramus, you are a donkey, Mr Danger ... You are a coward, a killer, a genocide, an alcoholic, a drunk, a liar." Other leaders had little time for Chávez's tirades. At a meeting of heads of state in 2007 the King of Spain publicly scolded Chávez, "Why don't you shut up?"

Hurling insults does little to enhance a leader's reputation in the world, but it draws attention, which populists and authoritarians typically crave. And although few may care about international respectability, they may enjoy projecting a sense of strength and self-confidence to their countrymen, for being seen to defy outsiders. Nearly two decades ago Robert Mugabe, Zimbabwe's then-president, sneered that Britain's prime minister, Tony Blair, was "a boy in short trousers", earning chuckles of approval even from his domestic opponents. Perhaps for similar reasons, Chinese diplomats have dismissed Justin Trudeau, Canada's prime minister, as a "boy". Another autocrat, North Korea's Kim Jong Un, called Donald Trump a "dotard" in 2017, though he did so in response to Mr Trump's own jibe, calling him "rocket man".

But even at the downright-rude end of the diplomatic spectrum, subtlety pays dividends. Crafty slights can be more scathing than crass ones. In 2010 Turkey and Israel had a diplomatic row because Israel's deputy foreign minister sat the Turkish ambassador on a low sofa at a meeting. In 2021 Turkey tried a similar trick by sidelining Ursula von der Leyen, the European Commission president, on a sofa while Mr Erdogan and Charles Michel, the president of the European Council, had a tête-à-tête in two big-boy chairs. And in 2007 Vladimir Putin, Russia's president, rattled Angela Merkel, then Germany's chancellor, by introducing her to his hulking black labrador, despite Ms Merkel's well-known phobia of dogs. He later claimed, "I wanted to do something nice for her."

Doubtless, barbs and insults will continue to fly. Indeed, modern diplomacy provides more opportunities than ever for new forms of bickering. Diplomats now trade memes on social media as put-downs and rebukes. In 2018, when the supreme leader of Iran sent a tweet referring to Israel as "a malignant cancerous tumour", Israel's embassy in America replied with a screenshot from *Mean Girls*, a film about gossipy high-school students. The caption read: "Why are you so obsessed with me?"

Why does electrification reduce political engagement?

Africa is the least electrified continent in the world. Nearly 600m people in sub-Saharan Africa – 53% of the total population – live in the dark. In May 2021 Cape Town was brought to a standstill by protests over a lack of electricity. Then, in November that year, South Africans engaged in politics through other means: by voting in municipal elections. Although South Africa is one of the most electrified countries in the region (85% of the population is connected to the grid) people there tend to be less politically active – that is, they protest less or are less likely to contact their local representative – than their regional neighbours. How does electrification affect political engagement?

Past studies have shown that increased provision of public services boosts political participation. People who send their children to public schools are more likely to campaign for a political party, for example. So access to reliable power should, in theory, also energise political engagement. Citizens have access to information online and, with electricity, can meet after sundown. But a recent study by researchers at Indiana University and Susquehanna University in Pennsylvania found that in sub-Saharan Africa switching on the lights makes people more likely to switch off politically.

The authors analysed public opinion surveys conducted by Afrobarometer, a pan-African research institution, taken between 2002 and 2015 and covering 36 countries. Respondents were asked if they lived in a neighbourhood connected to the grid and if they had recently taken part in any of three political actions: contacting a government official, voting in a national election, or taking part in a collective action such as attending a public meeting or marching at a protest. The researchers found that rates of political participation were, on average, 27% higher in non-electrified neighbourhoods than in electrified ones. The trend held when controlling for whether or not a country was a democracy.

Switching off

Sub-Saharan Africa, selected countries, 2014–15

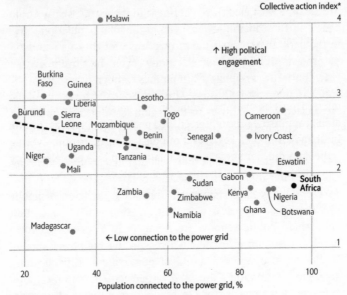

*A composite measure of various indicators of political participation

Source: "Does electricity demobilise citizens? Exploring access to the grid, political participation and democracy in Africa", by J. Brass et al., *Energy Research & Social Science*, 2021

But did access to electricity cause the dip in political activity, or was it merely correlation? Interviews that the researchers conducted in Ghana suggest the former. Once they had access to electricity, Ghanaians were more likely to stay at home – watching television, for example – instead of socialising with neighbours, where they might pick up news of problems in the community. And of course, with electricity, they may have felt more satisfied in their home lives and therefore less inclined towards activism. Some Ghanaians powered up without government help; they paid for their own street lights or purchased a private generator. That contributed to scepticism that an elected official was willing or able to meet their needs. The only exception to the trend, in Ghana and elsewhere in the region, was for people who were already involved in civil society, such as women's organisations. For them, living in an electrified neighbourhood was associated with increased political activity.

There are some caveats to the study. The Afrobarometer surveys did not ask about online activism, so not all political activity was captured by the questions. The questions about access to electricity referred only to national supplies, not personal generators (so didn't capture the privately electrified populations, such as the one in Ghana). And on a key aspect of political participation – voting – the data did not show a clear relationship between electricity and action. Still, the study suggests that rather than keeping their people in the dark, unpopular officials may benefit from turning on the lights.

What is the point of the Quad?

American diplomacy in Asia has been revving up. In September 2021 President Joe Biden announced a new security pact with Australia and Britain, known as AUKUS, to help Australia build nuclear-powered submarines. And later that month the leaders of America, Australia, India and Japan gathered in Washington, DC for the first in-person meeting of another grouping, the "Quad". Although its leaders had not previously sat down together, the group can trace its roots back to joint disaster relief after the Asian tsunami of 2004. Its communiqués talk of securing a "free, open, prosperous, rules-based and inclusive Indo-Pacific". But what really unites the four countries is the spectre of China and its growing muscle. What is the Quad, and what does it want to achieve?

After the initial co-operation on disaster relief, America, Australia, India and Japan met in 2007 for a "quadrilateral dialogue" on security matters. Many reckoned the new bloc would fizzle. India, once non-aligned and still suspicious of anything that smacked of an alliance, was non-committal, but in the end it was Australia, discomfited by China's prickly reaction, that was the first to abandon the group in 2008. Since then China has projected its power across Asia and the Pacific. And so, after the four countries' foreign ministers got together at a gathering of the Association of South-East Asian Nations in 2017, the Quad was reborn.

All four members have seen their relationships with China deteriorate. Chinese incursions around islands in the East China Sea that Japan controls, but that China claims, have grown ever more frequent. Australia has faced Chinese restrictions on all manner of exports, from wine to coking coal, following its call for an independent inquiry into the origins of the coronavirus pandemic. Indian and Chinese troops have clashed on their disputed border, resulting in the first fatalities in 45 years.

As a result, America has expanded its naval patrols in the South China Sea. In 2020 America, India and Japan invited Australia to rejoin their annual Malabar naval exercises after a 13-year gap, giving the Quad a de facto naval face (though India insists the Quad and Malabar are entirely separate). A Blue Dot infrastructure network, aimed by America, Australia and Japan at countering China's Belt and Road Initiative, promotes transparency and environmental sustainability (though India is yet to sign up). In March 2021 the Quad's leaders met for the first time, virtually, and agreed to expand vaccine manufacturing for South-East Asia. At their in-person meeting in September 2021 they discussed co-operation on the pandemic, climate change, infrastructure, emerging technologies and of course security. China's government, meanwhile, warned against forming "closed and exclusive 'cliques'" and said the Quad was "doomed to fail".

The Quad remains a work in progress. It has not yet really achieved all that much. It has certainly not stopped China from threatening its members. The promise of Asian vaccinations was predicated on supplies from India, which India's enormous second wave stymied. The importance of unofficial "Quad-plus" partners has also grown, as shown in the AUKUS deal (how it will work with the Quad remains to be seen) and growing British and French naval patrols in the Pacific. But in-person meetings of the Quad's leaders, like those held in September 2021 and May 2022, are statements of intent. China's hardening edge in military, diplomatic, economic and technological fields has given the group a renewed purpose.

Why are coups making a comeback?

A prime minister under house arrest, soldiers on the streets and a state of emergency declared. For Sudan it all felt like déjà vu. In the early hours of October 25th 2021 the country's military chief dissolved the transitional government, which had been sharing power between civilian and military leaders, and arrested most of the cabinet. Only a month earlier a similar attempt had been scuppered by the prime minister's henchmen. On its second attempt, the armed forces' takeover was successful. (The prime minister was briefly reinstated by the army in an effort to calm the country, but resigned six weeks later after soldiers brutally suppressed the protests.)

Sudan's government thus became the fifth to fall in 2021, according to a database compiled by researchers at the University of Central Florida and the University of Kentucky, who define a successful coup as one where the perpetrators hold power for at least seven days. The governments of Chad, Guinea, Mali and Myanmar had all been toppled earlier in the year. Between 2015 and 2020, there were just three successful oustings (and four failed attempts), but in 2021 coups made a comeback. More coups took place that year than in the previous five years combined.

That is bad news for the health of Africa's democracies. According to research by the Centre for Systemic Peace, an American think-tank, half of all forced regime changes between 2010 and 2020 resulted in greater authoritarianism and disorder. In 2019 massive protests led to the toppling of Omar al-Bashir, the dictator who ruled Sudan for 30 years, and a military coup. Yet many had hoped that Sudan was on a path towards democracy. Since the country's independence in 1956, there have been 16 attempted putsches. Only Bolivia and Argentina have seen more insurrections in the same period.

Countries in Africa are particularly vulnerable to putsches. Ailing economies and fragile institutions make coups more likely. The checks and balances that support democracy – such as electoral

Upwards putsch

Number of coups attempted worldwide, 1950–2021

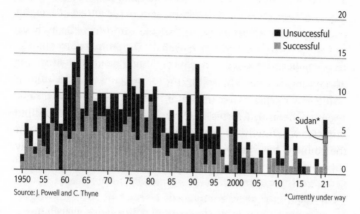

Source: J. Powell and C. Thyne

*Currently under way

commissions, independent courts and free media – are often too easily subverted. And instability begets instability: CoupCast, a coup-forecasting system operated by One Earth Future, an NGO, finds that the strongest predictor of future instability is past instability. It also finds that economic misery is linked to higher coup risk, as is extreme weather. The pandemic, and higher food and fuel prices as a result of the war in Ukraine, have increased the first; climate change is increasing the second. The relative dearth of coups in the past 15 years may have been a short-lived anomaly.

Do boycotts of sporting events work?

Sporting boycotts are almost as old as sport itself. In 332BC, the city of Athens threatened to withdraw from the ancient Olympics because of allegations of match-fixing against one of its athletes. In modern times boycotts have tended to be prompted by politics. In December 2021 America said its diplomats would not attend the 2022 Winter Olympics in Beijing, in protest against China's human-rights abuses against the Uyghur minority in Xinjiang. Australia, Britain, Canada and India followed suit, along with a handful of other countries, though their athletes still took part. The Chinese government dismissed America's announcement as "pure political grandstanding". Were these countries making an empty gesture? Or can boycotts be effective?

Boycotts are usually intended, at least in theory, to press governments into making some sort of political or social change – or to shame them. They rarely achieve much. For one thing, many boycotts that are threatened end up fizzling out. Before the Berlin Olympics in 1936, several countries considered withdrawing rather than be guests of Germany's Nazi regime. In the end 49 took part – the most at any Olympics until then. More recently, boycotts were mooted by Britain and Germany in the build-up to the football World Cup in Russia in 2018. But in the end, no teams stayed away.

Even widely observed and repeated boycotts often have little effect. Consider the mass sporting stayaways of the cold-war era. In 1980 America and 66 other countries and territories chose not to go to the Moscow Olympics, most in protest against the Soviet invasion of Afghanistan. The Soviet Union, along with other eastern-bloc countries, retaliated by boycotting the summer games in Los Angeles four years later. Neither gesture changed the dynamics of the cold war; they merely denied scores of athletes sporting glory. And some athletes went to Moscow anyway, despite their countries' official boycott. Similarly, the frequent refusals of Arab countries and Iran to compete against Israeli athletes have done little to resolve the Palestinian conflict.

But sometimes boycotts can work. Their most powerful endorsement comes from the anti-apartheid movement. For more than three decades, white-ruled South Africa was a sporting pariah. It was banned from all Olympics between 1964 and 1992 (largely because of pressure from other countries, rather than on the International Olympic Committee's initiative). And its participation in other sports such as rugby union and cricket was severely restricted. Many political scientists believe this sporting isolation contributed to the regime's downfall. According to one study in the book *How Sanctions Work*, published in 1999, it created pressure for change; another study, in the *Journal of Contemporary History*, suggests it undermined white racial ideology.

Why did this boycott work where others had failed? For a start, it was sustained long enough to hurt its intended target: white South African leaders, who cherished sport, and rugby and cricket especially. Nearly 75% of white South Africans in 1990 said they felt the impact of the sporting boycott strongly, according to one poll. The demands from the boycotters were also clear and specific, such as widening participation in sports to all races. Most important, the boycott was supplemented by a strong civil-society movement within South Africa, and by other sanctions from abroad, including economic penalties, which collectively exerted significant pressure on the country.

None of that applies in the case of China, which suggests that the diplomatic boycott of the winter games in Beijing was little more than symbolic. The sporting events still went ahead; China brutally suppresses any domestic protests against the regime; and America and other countries have strong economic links with China that they are unwilling to jeopardise. The diplomatic boycott did briefly amplify negative publicity about China's human-rights abuses, somewhat undermining its efforts to use the games to boost its "soft power" globally. Uyghur groups abroad welcomed this. But back in their homeland, nothing changed.

Why are eastern European countries cosying up to Taiwan?

When Taiwan opened a "representative office" in Vilnius, Lithuania's capital, in November 2021, it was the first new office opened by Taiwanese diplomats in Europe in 18 years. It is, in effect, an embassy, like Taiwan's other 28 offices in Europe. Unlike the others, however, it is allowed by its host country to use the name of Taiwan instead of Taipei, which is the name of the island's capital. As China sees it, this smacks of recognition by Lithuania that Taiwan is a separate country. China abhors any such notion. After Lithuania announced that it would host the representative office using the name Taiwan, China stopped approving export permits for Lithuanian producers and downgraded its diplomatic relations with the country, recalling its ambassador from Vilnius and ordering Lithuania's ambassador to leave Beijing.

Other central and eastern European countries have been cosying up to Taiwan too. In addition to Lithuania, the Czech Republic, Poland and Slovakia donated covid-19 vaccines to the island – the only EU countries to do so. One Taiwanese NGO coined the term #DumplingAlliance to celebrate the countries' shared values and love of meat-filled dough (the billions eaten in China each year notwithstanding). And in December 2021 representatives from Estonia, Latvia and Lithuania (among other countries) gathered in Taipei for the Open Parliament Forum, a summit designed to strengthen the island's relationships with the democratic world. So why are these eastern European countries so keen to build links with Taiwan?

History is one reason. The governments in many eastern European countries can trace their roots back to the anti-Soviet movements of the late 1980s and 1990s. Estonia, Latvia, Lithuania and Slovakia are all led by centrist or centre-right coalitions that are increasingly hawkish on China. Many see similarities between the Soviet Union, which once controlled them, and today's oppressive China.

But their concerns are not just historic. In the Czech Republic, for example, public opinion began to sour towards China in 2017 when it was accused by journalists and politicians of trying to interfere in Czech politics by dangling the promise of massive investments. Countries that border Belarus, such as Latvia and Lithuania, also worry about China's keenness to collaborate with Belarusian armed forces. Marcin Jerzewski of Taiwan NextGen Foundation, a Taipei-based think-tank, says there is a growing awareness in central and eastern Europe that Taiwan "is the best partner for sharing best practices against authoritarianism".

There are economic reasons too. Some of these countries have failed to reap much benefit from doing business with China. Between 2000 and 2019, Estonia, Latvia, Lithuania and Slovakia each received €100m ($113m) of foreign direct investment (FDI) from China, but this was far less than other European countries. Only 1% of Slovakia's GDP came from Chinese FDI, compared with nearly 7% of Germany's. Taiwan sees an opportunity. In October 2021 its National Development Council launched an investment tour of the Czech Republic, Lithuania and Slovakia, touting the scope for participation in high-tech industries such as semiconductors, in which Taiwan is a world leader.

China has not only denounced Lithuania for appearing to update Taiwan's status. It has also tried to portray the Baltic country as riddled with immorality. Zhao Lijian, China's foreign ministry spokesman, tweeted that Lithuania was beleaguered by racism, in particular in its treatment of Jews. It is true that some countries in central and eastern Europe are hardly exemplars of liberalism. Lithuania and Poland oppress their LGBT citizens, and Poland's government has weakened the country's democratic foundations, incurring the wrath of the EU.

But Taiwan has precious few friends. Only 15 countries formally recognise the island. And for all China's remonstrations, the ex-communist countries in Europe are far from joining that group. None of them has signalled any willingness to break off relations with the government in Beijing, which China would require were they to recognise Taiwan. But Lithuania has taken a step towards establishing a more normal relationship with the island, short of forging official ties. Some bigger countries, including America, are doing the same: Taiwan was invited to President Joe Biden's Summit for Democracy, which took place in December 2021. China, needless to say, was not.

What is China's hypersonic glide vehicle?

In August 2021 a Chinese Long March rocket streaked into space. That is hardly unusual; there were over 30 such launches in 2020. But having begun to orbit the Earth, the rocket's payload then swooped back down, glided through the upper atmosphere and crashed into the ground, missing a target by about 40km. According to the *Financial Times*, which first reported the news, this was a test of a new, nuclear-capable hypersonic glide vehicle. China has insisted that it merely conducted a "routine test of a space vehicle to verify technology of spacecraft's reusability". Yet the demonstration reportedly stunned American officials. "We have no idea how they did this," one of them told the newspaper. What are hypersonic gliders and why do they matter?

Conventional intercontinental ballistic missiles (ICBMs) follow a parabolic trajectory, like a ball thrown into the air that falls back down under the action of gravity. That makes them visible and predictable. A missile fired at America from either Russia or China must arc high over the North Pole, where it can be spotted by American and Canadian radar systems in the Arctic. And although some warheads can manoeuvre a little once they re-enter the atmosphere, it is easy to work out roughly where they are headed. China's unusual test, by contrast, appears to have involved two different technologies: orbital weapons and glide vehicles.

Orbital weapons, rather than going up and down in a parabolic arc, briefly enter orbit around the Earth. The Soviet Union operated such a weapon, the Fractional Orbital Bombardment System (FOBS), from 1969 to 1983 – "fractional" because it was not designed to circle the Earth repeatedly, as satellites do, but instead to drop from orbit after less than a full revolution. The advantage of this approach is that a warhead can travel around the Earth to America over the South Pole, thus bypassing existing radar shields. In recent years Russia has said it is building a FOBS-capable ICBM, and some think that the huge size of new North Korean missiles suggest a similar interest. China has long worried that American missile defences might undermine its relatively small, though apparently expanding, nuclear arsenal. The military drawback of orbital systems is that the rocket engines required to bring the warhead back into the atmosphere take up room, leaving less for nukes, and, when fired, they tend to be visible from to infrared sensors aboard American satellites.

Glide vehicles work differently. They are also lofted on a rocket but either are released in the upper atmosphere, before they ever get into space, or re-enter the atmosphere very quickly. Their design, with a high lift-to-drag ratio, means that they can then glide, unpowered, much farther than the re-entry vehicle of a normal ICBM warhead. They stay lower than either ICBM or orbital systems – thus hiding better from radar – and can take long and convoluted routes that avoid ground-based missile defences.

If descriptions of China's test are accurate, its significance would lie in the combination of these two technologies in a single weapon system. "China appears first in the world to combine an old concept of FOBS with modern glider technology," says Tong Zhao, a Beijing-based expert at the Carnegie Endowment, a think-tank. America has explored orbiting and glider technologies in its X-37B spacecraft, operated by the air force, says Mr Zhao, but "China appears the first to turn this combination … into a prototype strategic strike weapon." Even more astonishingly, the vehicle seems to have fired a missile while passing over the South China Sea at five times the speed of sound.

Joshua Pollack, editor of the journal *Non-Proliferation Review*, speculates that the weapon might be "multi-functional", with "the flexibility to evade defences in an unpredictable manner". America, he notes, has begun testing its Aegis missile-defence system, installed aboard dozens of warships, against ICBM targets in space. Orbital weapons and glide vehicles could dodge different interceptors in different ways, hedging China's bets. Another possibility is that Chinese gliders currently lack the range to take southerly polar routes without piggybacking on a FOBS-like weapon.

Missile defence may be much of the motivation for this new weapon. In 2002 America tore up the Anti-Ballistic Missile treaty with Russia and poured huge sums into anti-missile systems. Although American officials insist that these systems were designed to intercept North Korean and Iranian missiles, rather than Russian or Chinese ones, that was little consolation in Beijing. Chinese efforts may therefore be intended, in part, to ensure that the country's arsenal remains effective.

In which countries is corruption getting worse?

Most of the world scores poorly in Transparency International's annual corruption index. Using the assessments of business pundits and analysts, including figures from the World Bank and the World Economic Forum, the NGO scores countries from 0 to 100 based on perceptions of corruption in the public sector, with 100 indicating a squeaky-clean record. In the latest ranking, released in January 2022, almost 70% of countries score below 50. Poor countries tend to do worse than rich ones, partly because poverty makes corruption worse and partly because corruption makes poverty worse. The average score in sub-Saharan Africa is 33, the lowest for any region. In western Europe it is 66.

Some high-scoring democracies showed "significant deterioration" over the past year too – so much so that America dropped out of the 25 least corrupt countries for the first time. Blame Donald Trump's efforts to overturn election results in 2020, and the fact that conspiracy theories including QAnon are going mainstream. But the biggest drops were in countries whose governments muzzled the press and suppressed civil liberties under the cover of covid-19 prevention. Belarus dropped by six points relative to 2020, after a rigged election saw Alexander Lukashenko become president. The killing of human-rights defenders under Rodrigo Duterte in the Philippines, and the strangling of the free press in Nicaragua and Venezuela, contributed to reductions in the scores of those countries.

Improvements in the index are normally slow. Countries usually move by only a point or two from one year to the next, if at all. But regime change can prompt faster improvement: Armenia's score has risen by 14 points since 2017. Mass protests in 2018 swept away the political elite in favour of a government that has pressed charges against former high-ranking officials. More recently, though, Armenia's government has lost steam. In January 2022 the president resigned out of frustration over a lack of decision-making power. Angola's ten-point leap up the index over the same

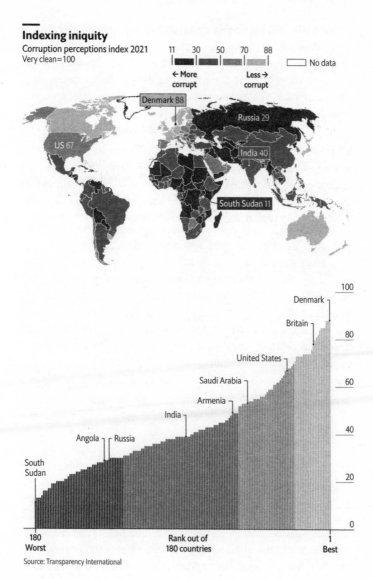

Indexing iniquity
Corruption perceptions index 2021
Very clean=100

← More corrupt   Less → corrupt

No data

Denmark 88
Russia 29
US 67
India 40
South Sudan 11

Denmark
Britain
United States
Saudi Arabia
Armenia
India
Angola   Russia
South Sudan

180
Worst

Rank out of
180 countries

1
Best

Source: Transparency International

period belies similar complexities. Though reforms since 2017 have pleased the IMF, most Angolans have yet to see much benefit.

Poor countries, especially those in Africa, the Middle East and Asia, are singled out in the report for the bad behaviour of their governments. Yet companies based in rich countries often facilitate corruption abroad. Transparency International publishes a separate report on countries whose companies bribe foreign officials – and the top scorers on that list are the same ones lauded as least corrupt by the organisation's main index. Countries vary in their enthusiasm for enforcing anti-bribery laws. Britain and Switzerland are among the "active" enforcers while Germany, Norway and Sweden are "moderate" ones, according to Transparency International.

Rich countries are not immune to influence-peddling. Owen Paterson, a former British MP who resigned after becoming embroiled in a lobbying scandal in November 2021, accepted at least £500,000 on top of his salary for consulting work and for lobbying on behalf of two companies. But he declared these payments in the register of MPs' financial interests, so media outlets were able to expose them through freedom of information requests. Politicians who demand bribes, buy votes or rig elections in poor countries are not so readily held to account.

A load of ballots: local politics around the world

Is political polarisation in America really rising?

Political wonks flocked to Seattle in October 2021 for the annual meeting of the American Political Science Association. Among other things, they discussed how political divisions hampered the fight against covid-19. America lagged behind much of the rich world in its vaccine rollout, in part because of the reluctance of some on the right to get jabbed. But the academic debate is not conclusive on the extent to which polarisation is rising; political scientists even disagree on how to define it. How is polarisation measured, and are American voters really growing further apart?

In general, political polarisation is defined as the grouping of people into two extreme positions. The tricky bit is determining which opinions or traits should be used to form those groupings. Polarisation can broadly be categorised in two ways, says Lilliana Mason of Johns Hopkins University. One category, "social polarisation", measures the extent to which a person's ideology and identity (which includes traits such as race or religion) are associated with their political party. High social polarisation results in increased partisan bias and negative feelings towards supporters of the other party. Nearly 40% of Americans, for example, would be upset if their child married someone who supported a party other than their own. The other category, "issue-position polarisation", measures the extent to which Americans' policy preferences reflect extreme positions rather than more moderate ones, irrespective of which party they support.

Depending on which definition you choose, polarisation trends look very different. Social polarisation has increased markedly over the past four decades. Starting after the second world war, and accelerating with the civil rights movement, ideological liberals and African-Americans shifted towards the Democratic party whereas conservatives and white Americans became increasingly Republican, on average – a process known as "sorting". Democrats have also become on average more urban, educated and female since the 1960s. When a person's social identity is more tied to their

Polarisation paradox
United States

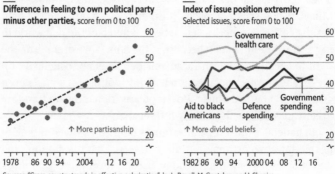

Difference in feeling to own political party
minus other parties, score from 0 to 100

↑ More partisanship

1978   86 90 94   2004   12 16 20

Index of issue position extremity
Selected issues, score from 0 to 100

Government
health care

Aid to black   Government
Americans   Defence   spending
spending

↑ More divided beliefs

1982 86   90   94   2000 04   08   12   16

Sources: "Cross-country trends in affective polarization", by L. Boxell, M. Gentzkow and J. Shapiro,
NBER Working Paper, 2020; "'I disrespectfully agree': the differential effects of partisan sorting
on social and issue polarization", by L. Mason, *American Journal of Political Science*, 2014

party affiliation, partisan bias grows. In 1978, Americans were 27
points colder toward voters from parties other than their own on a
100-point scale. The gap had grown to 56 points by 2020.

The same cannot be said for issue-position polarisation over
the same period. For instance, about half the population took a
moderate stance on abortion in 2016, a proportion that has held
steady since 1975. Across issues ranging from the armed forces to
government spending, the share of the population holding extreme
positions has not trended upwards nearly as much as social
polarisation, though it has increased somewhat since 2008.

Political scientists have several hypotheses for why partisan
sorting has occurred. One explanation is America's two-party
system, which makes it easier to form strong political identities
than in countries with several major parties, where holding views
that cross party lines is more common. Another is the growth of
media outlets that increasingly appeal to partisan viewpoints.
Fox News was started in 1996, and social polarisation accelerated
sharply in the years afterwards. Political scientists also point

to inequality and the growing population of racial minorities in America.

So has political polarisation grown in America? In one sense, yes. The link between someone's social identity, political ideology and party appears to be growing stronger. But when it comes to their actual positions on many issues, Americans have not moved apart to the same extent. The result is the paradox of polarisation: despite agreeing on much, Americans of different parties dislike each other more than ever.

Why does the LDP dominate Japan's politics?

Since its founding in 1955, Japan's Liberal Democratic Party (LDP) has dominated the country's politics. The party has ruled uninterrupted, save two brief stints in 1993–94 and 2009–12. Since regaining power in 2012, the LDP and its smaller coalition partner, Komeito, have won seven consecutive national elections, the most recent in October 2021. This political dominance comes not in an authoritarian system, but in a democracy with free and fair elections. How does the LDP keep such a firm grip on power?

The LDP emerged in the wake of America's post-war occupation of Japan and in the crucible of the cold war. After leftist forces united into a single Japan Socialist Party in 1955, Japanese conservatives, with a push from America's CIA, decided to merge the two main conservative parties: the Liberal Party and the Japan Democratic Party. The new LDP established the upper hand and went on to oversee Japan's economic growth miracle. It also benefited from a favourable electoral system skewed towards rural areas, where party influence was strong. Factions inside the party's big tent competed, with regime change coming from within; political pork helped grease the electoral wheels. This stretch of LDP dominance, known as the "1955 system", ended in 1993, when a group of LDP heavyweights broke with the party and formed an alternative coalition government with opposition parties. The renegade coalition disintegrated the next year, but not before making electoral reforms that paved the way for the subsequent emergence of the Democratic Party of Japan (DPJ), whose victory over the LDP in 2009 seemed to augur an era of true inter-party competition.

In power, however, the DPJ struggled to implement policies, alienated Japan's powerful bureaucracy and succumbed to infighting, changing prime ministers twice in three years. It also had the bad luck of being in charge in 2011 when an earthquake struck, triggering a tsunami and a meltdown at the Fukushima Daiichi nuclear power plant. The DPJ's shaky handling of the crisis set the stage for the LDP's resurgence. In the ensuing years, the opposition splintered; its current incarnation, the Constitutional Democratic Party (CDP), remains deeply unpopular and has struggled to shake off associations with the crisis. The LDP has also relied on its alliance with Komeito, which began in 1999, to retain power in recent decades. Komeito is the unofficial party of Soka Gakkai, a lay Buddhist group that has some 8m members across the country, and is especially strong in urban areas where the LDP is weaker. Allied with the LDP's extensive political networks throughout the country's 47 prefectures, that makes for a potent combination.

At least on the surface, the LDP's dominance has made Japan's politics seem more stable than those of other rich democracies, many of which have suffered from populism and extreme partisanship. But it has come with other costs. A lack of competition has made voters apathetic: turnout has fallen steadily in the past decade, a trend that suits the LDP just fine. It has also made politicians, and the LDP itself, less accountable to the public; in its leadership contest in September 2021, the party opted for Kishida Fumio, an inoffensive former foreign minister who satisfied the party's bosses but has limited popular support. Nor does the LDP's dominance signal satisfaction with the status quo. In a recent global study, the Pew Research Centre identified six countries where more than half the population wants "major changes or complete reform to the political, economic and health care systems": America, France, Greece, Italy, Japan and Spain. The LDP did lose some seats in the 2021 election. But until a viable alternative emerges and as long as its alliance with Komeito holds, the LDP's grip will remain secure.

What really happened on Bastille Day?

Many countries' national days mark important constitutional moments. America's dates to the signing of the Declaration of Independence on July 4th 1776; China's marks the official proclamation of the People's Republic on October 1st 1949. Not so in France. Bastille Day, celebrated on July 14th with a flurry of *tricolore*-waving and a grand military parade, instead celebrates a fairly chaotic mob riot.

On July 14th 1789 an angry crowd, spurred by famine, economic crises and years of government and societal corruption, set its sights on the Bastille fortress in the heart of Paris. It boasted 100ft-high walls and a wide moat, and had held high-profile prisoners including Voltaire, a writer and philosopher who was critical of the government. Until just a few days earlier it had held the Marquis de Sade, a libertine writer, who was then dispatched to a mental asylum. The imposing building had come to represent the injustices of France's *ancien régime*, and its storming was a blow against the monarchy and ruling class. The attack on the Bastille came to be seen as the start of the revolution that brought about the First Republic.

But it is strange that this date was picked as France's founding moment rather than, say, August 26th 1789, when the Declaration of the Rights of Man was adopted, or August 10th 1792, when the monarchy was suspended. And the event itself was not quite as glorious as the myth. The prison was scheduled for demolition anyway and held just seven prisoners. And despite perhaps being driven by a noble cause, the means of the attack were far from it. The prison's governor attempted to surrender to the crowd, but was torn to pieces and beheaded. Nonetheless, Bastille Day has been officially marked as France's founding moment since 1880. The government of the Third Republic, seeking to unify a demoralised country following the Franco-Prussian War of 1871, revived the commemoration as a grand military parade following its cancellation by Napoleon Bonaparte. July 14th may simply have been picked as the least controversial date to commemorate. Other options, such as the official founding of the First Republic on September 22nd 1792, could be seen as legitimising the Terror in the years that followed, when thousands of people were murdered.

The marking of Bastille Day over the past century and a half has been interwoven with France's tumultuous modern history. During the second world war it was all but cancelled in occupied France; instead Marshal Pétain, the Vichy governor, led a sombre wreath-laying ceremony. Charles de Gaulle, leader of the Free French, used the day to make a fiery speech in Congo in 1941, urging his compatriots to "be firm, pure and faithful". France's complex colonial history has also been felt on Bastille Day. On July 14th 1953, an anti-colonial demonstration by Algerians in Paris was met with shocking police brutality: seven people were killed and 50 injured. In 2014, the inclusion of several Algerian soldiers in the Bastille Day parade marking the first world war's centenary caused controversy in both countries. France's far-right National Front claimed that Algerians who had participated in the war had really been French, while in Algeria critics insisted that many soldiers had been forcibly conscripted during the war.

The complexities at the heart of Bastille Day echo the tensions in France's national identity: born of an idealistic yet violent revolution, and with a colonial past that it continues to struggle over. In 2021 several cities cancelled the festivities because of the pandemic. In Paris celebrations went ahead, including a military parade involving members of Takuba, a French-led European task force in the Sahel. The day remains an important show of national unity and military prowess, even if its actual history is rather less than glorious.

What is happening to the Uyghurs in Xinjiang?

Five years ago few people in the West had heard of Uyghurs. Since then they have become a focus of international criticism of China, which is accused of committing grave human-rights abuses against the Uyghurs and other ethnic groups in the country's far west. China's actions in Xinjiang, where most Uyghurs live, have prompted international sanctions, legal complaints and calls to boycott the 2022 Winter Olympics in Beijing. So who are the Uyghurs, and what is happening to them in Xinjiang?

The Uyghurs are a predominantly Muslim ethnic group native to Xinjiang, where about 11.6m of them live. Culturally and linguistically, they are more similar to Central Asians than to China's ethnic-Han majority. Uyghur is a Turkic language written in an Arabic script that has little in common with Chinese. Some Uyghurs reject the Chinese name "Xinjiang", meaning "new territory" and reflecting imperial-era conquest, for their native region. They prefer to call it "East Turkestan". In the first half of the 20th century two parts of the region, around the cities of Kashgar and Yining, declared independence from China. These attempts to break away failed, but they have not been forgotten by rulers in Beijing. Not all Uyghurs want independence, but the Chinese government views them with suspicion – all the more so since ethnic violence broke out in 2009 in Urumqi, the capital of Xinjiang, leaving a reported 197 Han and Uyghur people dead. In 2014 two violent attacks in Urumqi killed 34 people, fuelling the Communist Party's fears about terrorism in the region.

Around the time of the attacks in 2014, the Chinese government launched a "strike hard" campaign against terrorist violence in Xinjiang. There were two main strands: boosting surveillance of Muslim residents, and building internment camps to "re-educate" Uyghurs and other minorities deemed to show too much devotion to Islam or their culture. Behaviour that can lead to someone being rounded up includes having contact with foreigners or relatives overseas, observing Islamic practices, growing a beard, or anything else that might suggest the expression of a Uyghur rather than Chinese identity. The UN estimates that more than 1m people have been sent to the camps. Around one in ten Uyghurs has at some point been interned in one of them; for young and middle-aged men that rises to between a sixth and a third. According to former inmates and analysis of satellite imagery, prisoners are subjected to political indoctrination, forced labour, torture and forced female sterilisations. In 2019 the Chinese government said that it had released everyone from the camps, but satellite imagery showed that new camps were still being built in 2020.

Muslims in Xinjiang who are not interned face increased repression. In 2016 Xinjiang's police began monitoring Uyghurs using a data-collection system known as the Integrated Joint Operations Platform. It uses information from a range of digital and analogue sources, including surveillance cameras, mobile phones and medical histories. Young Uyghur women are put under pressure by Communist Party officials to marry Han men. The government sends Han civilians and officials to stay in Uyghur homes to act as "kin" – in other words, to spy. Uyghurs can be punished for contacting people in other countries. As a result their relatives abroad are often unaware of the sufferings of loved ones in their native land, including whether they have been detained in the gulag.

But they do know that life in Xinjiang has drastically changed. According to the Australian Strategic Policy Institute, a think-tank, 16,000 mosques in Xinjiang have been destroyed or damaged since 2017 – about 65% of the total. Just over half of those have been demolished. The government now imposes Mandarin-only education in schools and tightly controls any religious expression. China denies any human-rights abuses and says all these measures are necessary to prevent extremism. It says there have been no terrorist incidents in Xinjiang since 2017 and cites this as evidence that its policies there are effective. Most other observers would say that China is threatening the very survival of the Uyghurs' culture and identity.

What makes a failed state?

Afghanistan's ex-president, Ashraf Ghani, published a book in 2009 called *Fixing Failed States*. On August 15th 2021 he gave up trying to fix Afghanistan and fled to avoid capture by the Taliban, a jihadist group that seized power later that day. Afghanistan is often described as a failed state, perhaps the least-coveted accolade in geopolitics. However, it is not the only one. Pundits have lately applied the label to Myanmar, Lebanon and even Nigeria. But what does it mean? When does a state slide from fragility to outright collapse?

The term can be traced back to the 1990s. It was first used to describe Somalia, which crumbled into chaos after a coup toppled its dictator, Siad Barre, in 1991, and the country's clans started fighting among themselves. When fighters threatened aid workers, the United States sent troops to protect them. The Americans were then sucked into a battle in Mogadishu, the capital, that left 18 American soldiers and hundreds of Somalis dead (an episode described in the book *Black Hawk Down*, by Mark Bowden, and a film of the same name). The Americans gave up and pulled out. Somalia's collapse heralded the start of a post-cold war trend. Political crises soon followed in Bosnia, Liberia and Afghanistan. The Soviet Union stopped aiding client states after it ceased to exist itself. America stopped propping up dictators solely for being anti-Soviet (though many dictators found ways to keep the dollars flowing). Deprived of their deep-pocketed patrons, several regimes were toppled, and some states slid into anarchy.

The simplest definition of a failed state is one that cannot fulfil its most basic responsibility: to provide security. If the state can no longer provide security, and people start to take the law into their own hands, everything else breaks down, from electricity to roads, schools to health care. Most people in a failed state tend to be poor, whereas elites tend to be predatory. What is less clear is when a state moves from "failing" to "failed". Take Nigeria. Parts of the country seem perilously close to failure. Boko Haram, a brutal jihadist group,

Fragile States Index score
2021

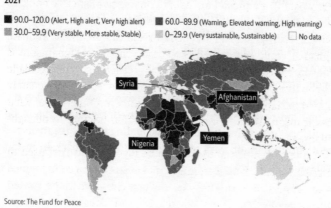

- 90.0–120.0 (Alert, High alert, Very high alert)
- 60.0–89.9 (Warning, Elevated warning, High warning)
- 30.0–59.9 (Very stable, More stable, Stable)
- 0–29.9 (Very sustainable, Sustainable)
- ☐ No data

Source: The Fund for Peace

controls a swathe of the north-east, and the army's attempts to crush it have proven ineffective. In other regions, conflicts between farmers and pastoralists kill thousands. Yet Nigeria holds together. Elections are dirty and violent, but more or less reflect the will of the people. Government is corrupt, but most Nigerians recognise it. When especially angry, many Nigerians describe their country as a failure. But it does not really deserve that label.

Yemen is a clearer example of state failure. Dozens of local groups have fought a ghastly civil war there since 2014. Unlike in Nigeria, the government has collapsed completely. Millions of people lack enough food. Massive destruction of health services and water infrastructure contributed in 2017 to one of the worst cholera outbreaks in recent history. Syria, too, is a failed state. There is no end in sight to its decade-long civil war. President Bashar al-Assad's regime rules the capital, Damascus. But much of the country is controlled by Islamists, remnants of the secular opposition, or Kurds, who have ambitions to secede. The economy is shattered. More than 600,000 Syrians are dead or missing; another 13m have fled their homes.

The Fund for Peace, an American think-tank, attempts to quantify how close a state is to failure in its annual Fragile States Index (see map on previous page). It scores every country from "Very sustainable" at best to "Very high alert" at worst, based on indicators including economic decline, security apparatus, public services, and human rights and the rule of law. Yemen and Syria both landed in the "Very high alert" category for 2021. So did Somalia. As for Afghanistan, before the Taliban takeover it was placed in the second-most-fragile category, "High alert". In Mr Ghani's book, he argued that upholding rule of law and ending violent insurgencies were two important ways to bring a failing state back from the brink. Alas, he failed.

How does Switzerland's referendum system work?

Switzerland's snow-capped mountains and pistes are among the more picturesque victims of global warming. The Swiss government spent two years coming up with a plan to cut carbon emissions, to meet its obligations under the Paris climate accords. The aim was to reduce net emissions to zero by 2050 by raising energy taxes, encouraging renewable power and so forth. But in June 2021 Swiss voters threw a spanner in the works, rejecting the government's plan in a referendum by 52% to 48%. It was one of 13 issues put to a referendum during the year. Among other proposals, voters rejected a national electronic ID and approved a "burqa ban" on facial coverings. The Swiss have the most pervasive system of referendums of any country in the world. How does it work?

Referendums are a form of "direct democracy", in which citizens vote directly on policy questions rather than allowing elected delegates to decide ("representative democracy"). In Switzerland their use dates back roughly to the origins of the modern state in 1848, when the country's relatively autonomous cantons were bound together into a federal republic. Unifying the cantons was difficult, with differences of language – French, German, Italian and Romansh – and religion. In 1847 Protestant factions defeated Catholic factions in a brief civil war. Several cantons began using referendums to approve laws, and in 1874 the system was introduced nationally in a new federal constitution. In effect, referendums were a concession to get a fissiparous population to countenance a modern central government.

There are three kinds of referendums under Swiss law. "Facultative" or "optional" referendums, such as that on the climate plan, approve or reject laws that have already been passed by the government, and can be called by getting 50,000 citizens to sign a petition (or by any eight of the 26 canton governments). "Popular initiatives", such as the burqa ban, are proposals to amend the constitution, and can be called with 100,000 signatures.

"Mandatory" referendums are required for constitutional changes or to sign international treaties. To be adopted, a popular initiative must win both a majority of votes nationally and a majority of votes in a majority of the cantons. In most cases a referendum is only the start of a long process: the government must work out legislation to implement the proposals.

Many reformers have admired Swiss direct democracy and the popular legitimacy it confers. The American socialist physician John Randolph Haynes looked to Switzerland when he campaigned for a referendum system in California. The state adopted it in 1911 and has been plagued by the consequences ever since, hamstrung by ill-thought-out popular mandates to keep property taxes low and refuse services to undocumented immigrants. In Switzerland, too, it is increasingly difficult to reconcile direct democracy with running a small modern state in the middle of Europe. In 2014 citizens passed a referendum demanding limits on immigration, which would have violated the country's treaties with the EU. After years of fruitless negotiation, the Swiss government settled for a modest employment preference for locals, and in a subsequent referendum voters rejected a proposal that sought tighter controls on immigration. Similarly, the rejection of the climate plan will simply force the government to design a new one. Eventually citizens may have to grudgingly accept a different version of the measures they tried to reject. That, too, is a kind of legitimacy.

How do Germany's elections work?

Nobody could ever quite replace *Mutti* ("mummy"), as Germans dubbed Angela Merkel, the country's chancellor since 2005, who announced in 2018 that she would not seek re-election in 2021. In quadrennial parliamentary elections held in September that year, Germans voted to elect her successor, and a new government. How exactly do Germany's elections work?

Germany is a federal parliamentary democracy in which the most powerful office is the chancellor. (As head of state, the president officially ranks higher, but the role is largely ceremonial.) The country is split into 299 constituencies, but the Bundestag, the lower house of the federal parliament, has at least 598 seats, and usually more. That is because every citizen has two votes. The first, *Erststimme*, is used to elect a local MP – roughly one representative for every 250,000 people. These votes are allocated using a first-past-the-post system, similar to Britain's Parliament, and every winning candidate is guaranteed a seat.

The second vote, *Zweitstimme*, is for a party rather than a candidate. This is used to determine the overall proportion of seats that each party holds in the Bundestag. These seats are assigned from a ranked list of candidates via proportional representation, providing the party has won at least 5% of the national vote. The 5% hurdle was designed to keep small, and often extremist, parties out of the Bundestag and to keep the government from splintering, as it did during the Weimar Republic in the 1920s and 1930s.

Why does the Bundestag's size vary? Its make-up has to reflect the results of the second vote. But it is common for voters to split their ballot, which means that parties often win more seats in the first vote than the second. If the proportion of constituencies won by a particular party in the first vote exceeds its share of the second vote, the extras are known as "overhang seats". Other parties are then awarded "balance seats" to keep the chamber proportionally representative of the second vote. The Bundestag elected in 2021, with 736 members, was the biggest ever. To keep its size in check

German parliamentarians voted in 2020 to reduce the number of constituencies from 299 to 280 by 2025.

Parties devise their lists for the second vote at their conferences several months ahead of the election. This is often where their candidate for chancellor is chosen too. Germany's government is usually a coalition. After the vote, talks get under way between parties and the new parliament is expected to convene within one month of the election. Whichever group of parties can command a majority gets to govern. Usually, the coalition party with the most seats fields the chancellor. After the 2021 election a "traffic light" coalition was formed by the Social Democratic Party (SPD), the Free Democratic Party and the Greens, whose party colours are red, yellow and green respectively. The SPD was the largest party in this coalition, and the party with the largest number of seats overall. Its leader, Olaf Scholz, became the new chancellor.

Why Britain needs more immigrants

Britain's population statistics paint a stark picture. The fertility rate, which can be thought of as the average number of children a woman will have during her lifetime, stands at 1.65 (far short of the replacement rate of 2.1). Life-expectancy projections are increasingly pessimistic too. Interim figures published in January 2022 by the Office for National Statistics (ONS) estimate that the population will increase by just 3% in the decade to 2030. In the decade to 2020 it grew by 7%. Meanwhile, the number of people aged 85 and over will rise sharply. In mid-2020 fewer than 2m people were in that age bracket. Projections suggest that by 2045 the number will be more than 3m.

As in other rich countries, women are having fewer children: after the sharp peak that followed the second world war, fertility rates have declined. And the big baby-boom generation is affecting demographics in Britain and beyond. In Japan, the *dankai no sedai* – those born between 1947 and 1949 – have contributed to the country's rapid ageing: almost 30% of the population are now aged over 65. The slowdown in life-expectancy increase is also weighing on Britain's population growth. Projections made since 2012 have steadily revised down period life expectancy at birth (a measure of the average number of years people will live beyond their current age). For someone born in 2025, the latest projected life expectancy is 2.1 years lower than the projection made in 2012.

This slow-growing, ageing population will impose costs. The number of adults of pensionable age for every 1,000 working-age people is projected to increase from 280 in mid-2020 to 341 by mid-2045. Other rich countries face even worse ratios: the European Union average for the same measure is projected to increase from 340 in 2019 to 590 in 2070. However reluctant they may be to do so, countries with ageing populations will have to look beyond their borders. Migration has been a key source of population growth in Britain for decades, but Ridhi Kashyap, a demographer at the University of Oxford, believes it will play an even more important

Boomer bust

Britain, demographics

Population age structure, '000

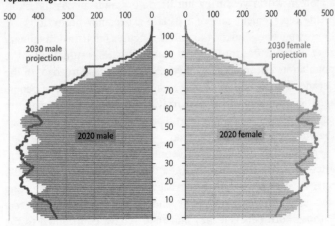

Life expectancy at birth*

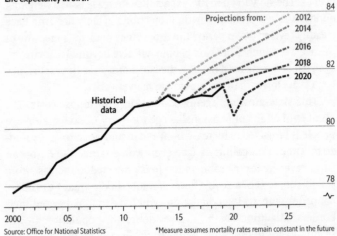

Source: Office for National Statistics   *Measure assumes mortality rates remain constant in the future

role in the future. "Given the grim mortality scenario and the revised downward estimates for fertility, migration is just becoming more salient," she says. All of this means anti-immigration governments are storing up trouble for the future.

How does the British monarchy's line of succession work?

"The only thing known to go faster than ordinary light is monarchy," mused Ly Tin Wheedle, the Confucius-esque philosopher in Terry Pratchett's *Discworld* novels. Because tradition demands that when a monarch dies, succession passes to the heir instantly, "there must be some elementary particles – kingons, or possibly queeons – that do the job". As soon as Queen Elizabeth II dies, her oldest son, Charles, will become the head of state of the four countries of the United Kingdom and more than a dozen Commonwealth countries, including Australia, Canada and Tuvalu. Everyone below him in the pecking order will move up a spot. An accession council made up of politicians, members of the privy council and other bigwigs would merely affirm his succession. How does Britain's royal line of succession work, and why might Charles's ascension to the throne seem different to his mother's?

The legal basis for succession stretches back to the 17th century and James II, the last Roman Catholic king of England. When Protestant bishops got the hump and invited William of Orange to invade, James fled to France. The throne went to his daughter Mary, a Protestant who had married William, and Parliament passed two acts: the Bill of Rights of 1689 and the Act of Settlement of 1701. These established that the monarch rules with the consent of Parliament, and set out numerous conditions that a successor must meet. A British monarch needs to be a descendant of Princess Sophia (the nearest Protestant heir to William of Orange, who became William III), and in communion with the Church of England. Until 2013, when Parliament passed a new Succession to the Crown Act, younger male heirs would jump ahead of their older sisters in line to the throne (Spain and Monaco's royal families still use this male primogeniture system), and anyone who married a Catholic was banned, even a dyed-in-the-wool Anglican.

Charles ticks all the boxes. As a result, on top of his mother's titles he would inherit the Duchy of Lancaster, a portfolio of assets, land and property worth around £577m ($797m), and a plum job as head of the Commonwealth, a club of 54 states, most of them former British colonies. His heir, William, would not be guaranteed this role, however. Commonwealth leaders agreed in 2018, at the behest of the queen, that the position would pass to Charles, but it is not hereditary.

In practice it may come to seem as though Prince William were already perched on the throne alongside his father. The oldest British monarch at the start of his reign was William IV, who took over in 1830 aged 64. Charles turned 73 in November 2021. And he is unpopular: a YouGov survey of 1,667 Britons in August 2021 found that 80% of people thought positively of the queen, and 78% approved of Prince William. Charles's approval rating was just 54%. The royal household may think it prudent for William to share the duties of head of state, both to prepare him for the big job and to make the monarchy seem younger and more dynamic. After the queen's record-breaking long reign, those mythical kingon and queeon particles, dormant for more than seven decades, may have to fly more frequently in future.

Why fewer Americans are trying to buy guns

America is the world's most heavily armed country, with a per-capita rate of gun ownership more than twice that of the runner-up (Yemen). Gun ownership has been rising steadily for years. But demand fluctuates in response to the political mood, mass shootings and other events. Sales spiked in spring 2020, as Americans worried that covid-19 lockdowns might presage stricter arms control and fretted about a broader breakdown in social order. Sales rose again that June, and the months following, during unrest after the killing of George Floyd, an unarmed black man, by a police officer. In 2020 and the first half of 2021 record numbers of people underwent the background checks required to purchase a gun legally. But the number of these checks dropped by an average of 16% per month between June and October 2021 compared with the same period a year earlier. By November they had dropped by 25%.

America has no national registry of guns. So the Federal Bureau of Investigation's National Instant Criminal Background Check System (NICS) is a widely used, though imperfect, proxy for demand. Licensed gun sellers use the NICS (or state-based equivalents) to determine whether potential buyers have criminal or other records that would make them ineligible to purchase a firearm. Small Arms Analytics & Forecasting (SAAF), a research consultancy, calculates that 1.7m guns were bought in November 2021, a 21% drop from the record 2.1m in the previous November. (These numbers are based on an adjustment of the NICS numbers that excludes checks unlikely to lead to gun sales, but that does not capture all private sales by unlicensed sellers. The true sales figures are likely therefore to be higher.)

Though sales remain higher than pre-pandemic levels, declines are occurring across all states studied, each of which has its own laws governing background checks. An analysis by the SAAF's chief economist, Jurgen Brauer, and *The Economist* shows a median 31% drop for handgun sales and 20% for long guns in states won

For whom the gun boom booms less
United States, handgun background checks by state*
Jun–Nov 2021, % decrease on a year earlier

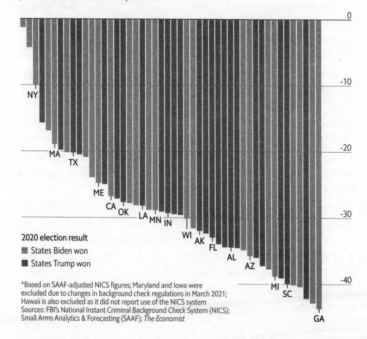

2020 election result
■ States Biden won
■ States Trump won

*Based on SAAF-adjusted NICS figures; Maryland and Iowa were
excluded due to changes in background check regulations in March 2021;
Hawaii is also excluded as it did not report use of the NICS system
Sources: FBI's National Instant Criminal Background Check System (NICS);
Small Arms Analytics & Forecasting (SAAF); *The Economist*

by Donald Trump in the 2020 election, and reductions of 27% for handguns and 17% for long guns in states won by Joe Biden. Why have sales slowed?

Concerns about the breakdown of law and order during the pandemic have calmed, reckons Timothy Lytton, an expert on the American gun industry at Georgia State University. The surge in sales was driven by two types of worry, he says. Some people who support gun rights were worried about the government growing too big through mandates, such as lockdowns, that restricted individual liberty. First-time buyers, by contrast, may have been concerned about the government not being big enough to protect them. But now, he says, "there has been a lowering of anxiety around the pandemic." As a result, both groups are buying fewer guns.

Climate matters: environmental concerns and curiosities

Why beef is the new coal

Few dishes whet more palates than a juicy cut of beef. One poll in 2014 found that steak was Americans' favourite food. Unfortunately, by cooking so many cows, humans are cooking themselves too. The impact of food on greenhouse gas (GHG) emissions can slip under the radar. In a survey in Britain in 2020, the share of respondents saying that "producing plants and meat on farms" was a "significant contributor" to climate change was the lowest among ten listed activities. Yet two papers published in 2021 in *Nature Food* find that food, especially beef, creates more GHGs than previously thought. Forgoing steaks may be one of the most efficient ways to reduce your carbon footprint.

In 2019 the UN's Intergovernmental Panel on Climate Change estimated that the global food system was responsible for 21–37% of GHG emissions. In March 2021 researchers from the European Commission and the UN's Food and Agriculture Office released a study with a central estimate near the top of this range. It attributed 34% of GHGs produced in 2015 to food. This elevated share stems in part from accounting choices. The paper assigns the full impact of deforestation to the agriculture that results from it and includes emissions after food is sold (such as from waste and cooking). But even when the authors excluded embedded emissions from sources like transport and packaging, they still found that agriculture generated 24% of GHGs. According to the World Resources Institute, a research group, the world's cars, trains, ships and planes produce a total of 16%.

Another paper, by Xiaoming Xu of the University of Illinois at Urbana-Champaign and eight co-authors, allocates this impact among 171 crops and 16 animal products. It finds that animal-based foods account for 57% of agricultural GHGs, versus 29% for food from plants. Beef and cow's milk alone made up 34%. Combined with the earlier study's results, this implies that cattle produce 12% of GHG emissions. Relative to other food sources, beef is uniquely carbon-intensive. Because cattle emit methane and need large

Annual emissions from animal- and plant-based foods
CO₂-equivalent gigatonnes from ten biggest sources, 2010

● Animal-based ● Plant-based

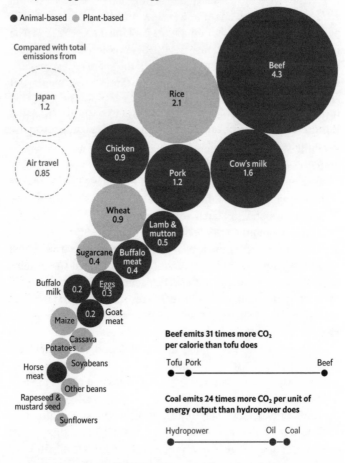

Compared with total emissions from

Japan 1.2

Air travel 0.85

Beef 4.3

Rice 2.1

Chicken 0.9

Pork 1.2

Cow's milk 1.6

Wheat 0.9

Lamb & mutton 0.5

Sugarcane 0.4

Buffalo meat 0.4

Buffalo milk 0.2

Eggs 0.3

Maize 0.2

Goat meat

Cassava

Potatoes

Soyabeans

Horse meat

Other beans

Rapeseed & mustard seed

Sunflowers

Beef emits 31 times more CO₂ per calorie than tofu does

Tofu Pork   Beef

Coal emits 24 times more CO₂ per unit of energy output than hydropower does

Hydropower   Oil Coal

Sources: "Food systems are responsible for a third of global anthropogenic GHG emissions", by M. Crippa et al., *Nature Food*, 2021; "Global greenhouse gas emissions from animal-based foods are twice those of plant-based foods", by X. Xu et al., *Nature Food*, 2021; M. Heller et al.; J. Poore and T. Nemecek; M. Pehl et al.; Quantis; World Resources Institute; IPCC; Our World in Data

pastures that are often created via deforestation, they produce seven times as many GHGs per calorie of meat as pigs, and about 40% more than farmed prawns. This makes beef a bigger outlier among foods than coal is among sources of electricity: burning coal generates just 14% more GHGs than burning oil, another common fuel.

These figures may understate the environmental benefits of shrinking the cattle population. Methane dissipates relatively fast, meaning that past bovine emissions soon stop warming the planet if those animals are not replaced. Such a change could also raise the output of plant-based foods, by making land now used to grow animal feed available for other crops. It takes 33 plant calories to produce one calorie of beef. The simplest way to cut beef output is for people to eat other animals instead, or become vegetarians. But convincing carnivores to give up their burgers is a tall order. Fortunately, plant-based imitation meats (such as the Impossible burger) are becoming far more convincing, and lab-grown meats have started to move from laboratories to high-end restaurants. Doing without beef from live cattle is hard to imagine, but the same was true of coal 100 years ago. Alternatives to meat could play an essential role in staving off a climate catastrophe.

What really goes on during COP climate negotiations?

Climate conferences, known as COPs, happen each year. The name is a wholly uninspired acronym for "Conference of the Parties", meaning signatories to the United Nations Framework Convention on Climate Change. But not all COPs are equal. When the Paris agreement was signed in 2015, it was agreed that every five years countries would return with more ambitious plans to reduce their greenhouse gas emissions and tackle global warming. Such events are known as "big COPs". The events held in the intervening years, known as "small COPs", tend to focus on laying the groundwork for negotiations as the bigger events. Because the coronavirus pandemic caused COP to be cancelled in 2020, the most recent big COP was COP26, held in Glasgow in November 2021. How does climate diplomacy at these events really work?

COP26 began, as all COPs do, with a ceremonial opening plenary. That was followed by two days of world leaders on stage talking about climate change, concentrating either on what their countries intended to do about it (if rich) or on the dire consequences they face (if poor). After this, the remaining days of a COP typically have themes – such as finance and energy – and see politicians and business leaders stepping up to announce various new pledges, coalitions and projects. Outside the doors, activists rage against superficial commitments and rally against political inaction.

Despite the well-publicised hoopla, much of the action occurs off-stage. Once heads of state leave, members of each country's delegations begin negotiating, drafting papers that set out their positions on various issues. These meetings should be watched over by accredited observers – normally from civil-society groups like NGOs, and from the developing countries most affected by climate change – who are meant to hold decision-makers to account. In 2021, to much annoyance, almost all observers were shut out of the negotiating rooms because of covid-19 restrictions.

The draft texts are written in the strange, sterile language of international diplomacy and an inordinate amount of time is spent on wording: debates on whether something "should" or "will" happen can stretch out for days. They also end up littered with square brackets, which denote areas where there is significant disagreement. For example, the text for Article 6 of the Paris agreement – a controversial clause about global carbon markets – began COP26 with 373 bracketed sections, after talks failed to reach any consensus on it at COP25 in Madrid in 2019.

By the start of the second week, delegates hand over proposals to their ministers and lead negotiators. The real haggling now begins, and arguments rumble on for the rest of the conference. The aim is to draft a document on which all countries agree: a big task and one that sometimes results in disfiguring compromises. In Copenhagen in 2009, after talks broke down in acrimony, the final statement did little more than recognise the scientific case for limiting global warming (no commitments to reduce emissions were achieved). The process can bring hardened diplomats to tears. In Bali in 2007, after almost a fortnight of squabbling, Yvo de Boer, the diplomat in charge of the summit, wept while trying to tell delegates of the importance of reaching an agreement.

Negotiations normally continue until the last possible moment, often stretching into the wee hours of the final weekend. The hosts scuttle between warring factions, trying to smooth over countries' concerns. Eventually some kind of accord is read out at the final plenary. Some countries celebrate; others point fingers at those they think haven't done enough. COP26 ended with an accord that was generally regarded as disappointing. At the last minute, India demanded that a crucial clause on reducing coal usage be watered down. However, countries did commit themselves to further accelerating their decarbonisation plans and, specifically, to strengthening their emissions-reduction targets for 2030 in time for the event in 2022, rather than at the "big COP" due in 2025. COP27, to be held in Egypt in November 2022, will therefore not be big, or small, but a medium-sized COP.

Why is India still so dependent on coal?

In the final minutes of the COP26 climate conference held in Glasgow in November 2021, with a deal in sight, India hit the pause button. With the backing of China and a few other countries, it insisted on replacing a commitment to "phase out" the use of coal power with a pledge merely to "phase down" its use. This one-word shift has potentially big implications. The phase-out promise had been seen as an important step towards ridding the world of its filthiest fuel. India knows the cost of coal. Particulate emissions from burning the stuff kill 112,000 Indians each year, by one estimate. With this in mind, India has ramped up investment in renewable energy: over the past decade, its capacity has more than quadrupled. So why does it still burn so much coal?

The first reason is that it needs to keep the lights on. India's population, currently 1.4bn, is growing and electricity use is soaring. India needs to add capacity equivalent to all the EU's output over the next 20 years, according to the International Energy Agency. Today 70% of the country's electricity comes from coal. The government has promised to increase renewable-energy capacity to 500 gigawatts by 2030, more than doubling the current output. But even this increase would still account for just half of anticipated need. The creaking electricity grid needs an upgrade too. Distribution companies, straddled with a collective debt of $80bn, are ill equipped to make the investments required to store and transmit renewable energy reliably. That makes solar power, an apparently obvious solution for India, harder to implement at scale.

Other countries also dread the prospect of unmet energy demand, which could stunt economic growth. That is why China joined India in pushing for a mere phase-down of coal, a rare moment of solidarity in an otherwise bristly relationship. The two countries are united by a sense of historical injustice. Their leaders feel that the West, after blazing through mountains of coal on its way to becoming rich, is unfairly trying to prevent them from doing the same. Indians, especially, feel hard done by. Though India is the world's second-biggest consumer of coal, on a per-person basis it burns a little more than a third of what America does.

India has another reason for hanging on to coal: politics. The black stuff is big business, making it ripe for corruption. In the 1990s and 2000s mining contracts were handed out to government cronies at knockdown prices, a scandal that became known as "Coalgate". Mining also provides a rich seam of votes. According to one study, 10m–15m Indians depend on coal for their livelihoods, many of them miners in the country's poorest states, Jharkhand and Chhattisgarh.

All this makes it fiendishly difficult to scrub coal from India's economy. But more could be done. For a start, India could refurbish existing plants to burn coal more cleanly. Better distribution infrastructure would enable it to exploit its solar potential more quickly. That would still leave the workers who depend on coal mining. At some point the rosy projections that have India clamouring for more energy ought to provide them with new and better job opportunities – and the luxury of planning a healthier future for their children.

What is the "3.5% rule" beloved of climate protesters?

Extinction Rebellion (XR), a global environmental movement that specialises in disruptive protests, says it needs "the involvement of 3.5% of the population" if it is to succeed in achieving its aims. That is still some way off: in Britain that would amount to around 2m people. The 3.5% figure sounds both arbitrary and strangely precise. So where does it come from, and what is so special about that figure?

The "3.5% rule" comes from Erica Chenoweth, a political scientist at Harvard University, who found it was a useful predictor of a protest's success. She posits that no government can stand up to that share of the population mobilising against it. Ms Chenoweth proposed it in 2013, after studying 323 violent and non-violent protests that occurred between 1900 and 2006 worldwide. In every case, when at least 3.5% of the population attended a "peak" event, such as a mass gathering, they achieved their aims. One example was Georgia's Rose Revolution in 2003. More than 180,000 protesters (equivalent to 4.7% of the country's population) gathered outside the parliament to oust President Eduard Shevardnadze, a strongman left over from the Soviet era. Protesters handed out roses to soldiers, who lowered their weapons. Shevardnadze was removed from power without bloodshed.

It is not always that simple. In 2019, some 2m Hong Kongers – more than a third of the city's population – took part in a demonstration against plans to bolster extraditions to mainland China. In the years since, the clampdown by Hong Kong's authorities has only intensified. There are caveats too. Non-violence tends to work better than violence. Ms Chenoweth's research showed that serious political change occurred 53% of the time after peaceful protest compared with 26% after violent protest. Peaceful demonstrations present fewer physical barriers to participation: children, disabled people and the elderly can join a march, whereas riots are generally started by physically fit young men. Non-violence is also more likely to win sympathy from security forces.

Climate protesters are often disruptive but rarely violent. But the 3.5% rule may not be compatible with their demands. Ms Chenoweth's research accounts only for "maximalist" movements with clear goals, such as regime change or territorial independence. The demands of climate activists, by contrast, are often vague. XR's website lists the group's three main demands of world governments: "Tell the truth", "Act now" and "Go beyond politics". Moreover, global warming tends to attract protesters globally. In 2019, 4m people marched in protest at rising temperatures, many of them teenagers inspired by Greta Thunberg's school strikes. In one country, that number would be difficult for any government to ignore. But spread across the world the impact was weakened.

That does not make climate protests useless if they fail the 3.5% test. After the climate demonstrations in 2019, internet searches for "climate change" surged worldwide. Public awareness makes politicians pay attention. And smaller, more extreme protests may act as a radical flank that increases the political leverage of moderates, who come to be seen as a more palatable alternative by lawmakers. XR and other environmental movements may see the 3.5% rule as an important predictor of success, but it isn't the only one.

How much farmland would be needed if everyone were vegan?

Many vegans restrict their diet to reduce animal suffering. But many also do so for environmental reasons. Eliminating meat, fish, dairy and eggs would reduce emissions. Producing a prime steak or vintage cheese, for example, involves feeding the animals that produce meat and dairy products with plants, rather than consuming those plants directly. Beef farming produces 31 times more CO_2 emissions per calorie than tofu production does, and eating beef delivers only 5% of the calories that go into producing it.

That inefficiency means that humans need to grow more plants than they would in a purely vegan world. For all the spread of veganism and the growing popularity of "veganish" partial alternatives, such as Veganuary (going vegan just for January), meat-eating is increasing globally. Its geography and composition are changing too. China's appetite for its favourite meat – pork – appears to have peaked; beef is becoming more popular. India, which eats very little beef, is drinking more milk. Africa, with its fast-growing population, will demand more meat in future. Already, of all habitable land, half is used for agriculture, according to the UN Food and Agricultural Organisation. Of that, about 80% is dedicated to pasture or crops for animal feed, according to Joseph Poore and Thomas Nemecek, the authors of an extensive study of global food systems (see chart opposite).

The research comes with considerable uncertainty. Although it compiles data from 38,700 farms and 570 studies, mapping the environmental impact of food production is difficult and imprecise. Roughly half of the data predate 2010, for instance. But the study gives a sense of what land use could look like, if diets changed radically.

If everyone were vegan, agriculture would need just a quarter of the land it uses today. Even a diet avoiding only meat from cattle and sheep would cut land use in half. What might that surplus space be used for? Quadrupling food production is not a viable option. Some

Food for thought
Share of habitable land, %

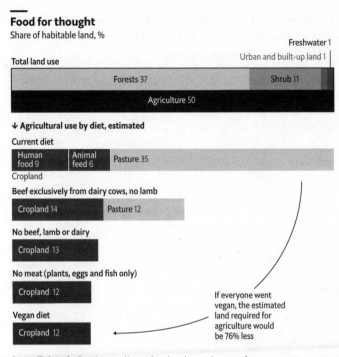

Sources: "Reducing food's environmental impact through producers and consumers",
by J. Poore and T. Nemecek, *Science*, 2018; UN Food and Agriculture Organisation; Our World in Data

current pastureland, for example in the Scottish highlands, could not be converted to high-yield cropland. But in most places where agriculture is currently expanding, such as the Amazon rainforest in Brazil, a shift from animal to plant production would mean more food per acre. Surplus farmland could also be used for other purposes, such as forestry, or restored to rainforest.

Some may worry about the cultural impact. Eliminating meat production would change landscapes, ways of life and relationships with animals and food shaped over millennia – and parts of economies linked to them, including tourism. But such concerns do not apply as readily to land cleared to produce ever more burgers to be consumed thousands of miles away. A wholescale shift to veganism is unlikely. But these models suggest a little more Veganuary spirit all year round would be a good thing.

Why pumping groundwater isn't a long-term solution to drought

Signs of drought have proliferated across the American West in the past two decades. One analysis suggests that it is the worst "megadrought" for 1,200 years. California has been forced to ration water for farmers in the state's Central Valley. Salmon are dying en masse in the Pacific Northwest as river temperatures climb. Lake Mead, on the border of Nevada and Arizona, is drying up. The country's largest reservoir is so depleted that the Bureau of Reclamation, an agency within the Interior Department, declared the first ever water shortage for the Colorado River in August 2021. Facing cuts to their supplies of surface water, some farmers in the region have been pumping more groundwater. Is pumping a sustainable way to weather the drought?

Groundwater is stored in aquifers (bodies of porous rock) that can be tapped by wells and used for drinking water or irrigated agriculture. Groundwater is the source of drinking water for half of Americans, and nearly all of the country's rural communities. Worldwide, about 70% of the groundwater pumped is used for agriculture. The problem is that groundwater has become dangerously depleted in places where pumping has exceeded the rate at which aquifers are naturally replenished.

An analysis from the United States Geological Survey in 2013 found that between 1900 and 2008, groundwater was depleted by 1,000 cubic kilometres nationwide, or about twice the volume of Lake Erie, one of North America's Great Lakes. A quarter of that was lost after 2000. The regions where depletion was most severe were the high plains, the south-west and the Gulf coast. America isn't alone. More than half of the world's population lives in countries where aquifers are overpumped for crop irrigation. Groundwater depletion can also cause the earth to sink slowly, a phenomenon known as land subsidence. As the ground settles, aquifers lose some of their storage capacity. In coastal regions subsidence can also contribute to rising sea levels.

In America, states eventually began to recognise overpumping and legislate against it. Arizona passed a law regulating groundwater use in 1980. To its chagrin, California's state government did not do so until 2014. In many cases, farmers could replace their groundwater use with water from rivers. A massive, costly aqueduct carrying Colorado River water to cities and farms in thirsty central Arizona was completed in 1993. But rather than encouraging judicious use of water, says Newsha Ajami, a hydrologist at Stanford University, the added supplies helped farmers in California increase their acreage. "Eventually it became, oh, we have groundwater. And on top of that, we have this surface water that's coming. So let's just make the best out of these two resources," she says.

Now the tables have turned. Reservoirs across the region are drying up. Farmers in Arizona were among the first to see cuts to their share of Colorado River water in January 2022. Some may have returned to pumping to keep yields high. Many rural areas in the Grand Canyon State are not covered by the law from 1980, which focused on cities. Policymakers are exploring ways to replenish groundwater more quickly, known as "artificial recharge". But that takes time. Meanwhile, the West keeps on getting drier.

What would a world powered entirely by offshore wind look like?

Energy shortages and high prices, driven by the economic rebound of 2021 and exacerbated by the war in Ukraine, mean that countries around the world are taking a closer look at investment in renewable sources. In October 2021 Deb Haaland, America's secretary of the interior, announced plans to open up huge sections of America's coastline for offshore wind-farm development. These new turbines could, according to government estimates, generate as much energy per year as 30 new conventional nuclear-power plants. In Britain, meanwhile, plans announced in March 2022 call for a tripling of solar capacity and a fivefold jump in offshore wind capacity by 2030. Wind is a clean and renewable source of electricity. Putting noisy turbines offshore reduces the amount of disturbance they cause to people. And they are often far enough out to sea not to spoil ocean views. But just how much shoreline would be required to produce all the power the world needs?

The total amount of energy needed to power the world for one year is around 556 exajoules (556 followed by 18 zeros). A single square kilometre of wind turbines produces roughly 80 terajoules (that's 80 with 12 zeros) each year. That means around 7m square kilometres of offshore farms would be needed to power the whole world. Projecting this area onto a map of the world's wind-power density – a measure of wind speeds – *The Economist* worked out the optimal locations for these imaginary installations, using some of the same data as Land Art Generator, a public arts initiative. Locations are scattered around the globe. Some dot the west coast of America, one of the sites proposed by the Biden administration. Others cluster in the North Sea, where many of the world's most productive wind farms are already installed.

Wind will never be the sole source of the world's energy. Wind farms are only effective in certain places and even then the output is intermittent, somewhat unpredictable and impossible to control. Offshore wind is also one of the most expensive forms of renewable

Winds of change
Optimal location of offshore wind farms needed to supply the world's total energy demands

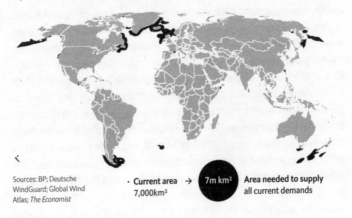

Sources: BP; Deutsche
WindGuard; Global Wind
Atlas; *The Economist*

· **Current area** → 7m km² **Area needed to supply**
7,000km²   all current demands

energy. Wildlife campaigners complain that the spinning blades can be deadly to birds and that underwater construction disturbs sealife (although turbine bases can also create artificial reefs, which promote biodiversity).

A more realistic prediction is that in a net-zero world, in which there is an overall balance between the amount of greenhouse gases emitted into the atmosphere and the amount removed, 7.5% of the world's energy will come from offshore wind farms. If this were to happen overnight it would mean increasing the number of square kilometres of offshore wind installations from roughly 7,000 currently in operation to 525,000. Hardly a breeze.

What is La Niña?

It was an Australian summer that didn't look like the postcards. In October 2020, giant hailstorms struck south-eastern Queensland, hammering some suburbs with stones the size of cricket balls. March 2021 brought the worst floods in half a century to New South Wales. At least two people died and over 20,000 were evacuated. Hundreds of homes in western Sydney were subsumed as rivers broke their banks. These violent weather conditions were fanned by a weather phenomenon known as La Niña. And in November 2021, Australia's Bureau of Meteorology (BOM) rained on Aussies' summers by declaring that it was happening for the second year in a row. The World Meteorological Organisation confirmed it too. The BOM predicted this La Niña would be weaker than the last, enduring "until the late southern hemisphere summer or early autumn 2022". But what is La Niña?

Spanish for "little girl", La Niña is the less famous counterpart of El Niño, a temporary warming pattern. Together they form one of the world's most important weather-making phenomena. The El Niño–Southern Oscillation (ENSO) sloshes back and forth across the Pacific Ocean every few years, changing the temperature of surface waters and the state of the atmosphere as it does so. In "normal" years, trade winds blow west along the equator, pushing warm surface water from the Americas towards Asia. To replace it, cold currents surge upwards from the depths in the eastern Pacific. In El Niño years this is partly reversed, and warm water spreads back towards South America. La Niña years, by contrast, exaggerate the normal pattern. The winds blow harder than usual, causing warm water to pool around Asia, while surface temperatures across the rest of the Pacific fall. They must slip by 0.8°C below the average for Australia to deem it a La Niña. Other countries have different thresholds for declaring La Niña: America's National Oceanic and Atmospheric Association (NOAA) said that one had already developed in October 2021.

The effects can be devastating to regions throughout the tropics.

A strong La Niña brings destructive storms to Australia and parts of Asia, because heat and moisture rise off warm waters, forming clouds, then rain. During La Niña in 1998, flooding in China killed thousands and displaced over 200m people, and over half of Bangladesh's landmass was subsumed. Outside Asia, La Niña has the opposite effect: it fuels droughts (as well as sometimes floods) in parts of Africa and the Americas. A collapse in food production triggered by La Niña in 2011 was followed by a famine in Somalia which killed 260,000 people and left 10m people in the Horn of Africa hungry. In 2021, wilting crops in the southern United States and Brazil forced up global food prices; by reducing the amount of electricity generated by Brazilian hydroelectric dams, La Niña also contributed to the spike in natural-gas prices. La Niñas can wreak havoc on commodity markets too. A cyclone that struck Australia in 2011 closed or restricted the output of 85% of Queensland's coal mines and destroyed sugar-cane crops, sending sugar prices to 30-year highs.

What of climate change? La Niña temporarily cools global average temperatures and masks the warming caused by emissions of greenhouse gases. For instance, 2021, one of the hottest years on record, would have been warmer without the cooling effect of two back-to-back La Niña events. Climate change may also alter ENSO cycles. There is nothing unusual about consecutive La Niñas: of the 12 "first-year" examples recorded by the NOAA since 1950, eight were followed immediately by a second. However, some scientists predict that La Niña and El Niño will become more severe as global temperatures rise. Research published in 2020 by the American Geophysical Union concluded that "under aggressive greenhouse gas emission scenarios", extreme Niñas and Niños may double in frequency. That means people around the world, not just around the Pacific, will have to pay more attention to them.

What are "nationally determined contributions" to curb climate change?

In April 2021 President Joe Biden announced a plan to cut America's greenhouse gas emissions in half by 2030, compared with their levels in 2005. That is nearly twice the reduction promised by Barack Obama in 2015 (and later cancelled by Donald Trump). Other countries have announced similar pledges, known as "nationally determined contributions" (NDCs), which are a crucial part of the global framework to tackle climate change. But what exactly are they?

The concept of NDCs was first introduced at COP19, the UN climate summit held in Warsaw in 2013. At first they were vague. Governments that were "ready to do so" were invited to submit non-binding climate pledges to the United Nations Framework Convention on Climate Change (UNFCCC) by the first quarter of 2015. Crucially, these pledges were to be formulated by countries based on their own priorities, needs and prospects. This flexibility was meant to overcome the problems that had plagued the Kyoto Protocol, the UNFCCC's first accord, which came into force in 2005. That had committed only developed countries, such as Britain, to cutting their emissions. Developing countries, including China – which, by 2006, was the largest emitter of carbon dioxide in the world – were not included. This arrangement was deemed to be too rigid and unfair. America ultimately refused to ratify it, and Canada withdrew in 2011.

A tricky balancing act ensued: NDCs needed to contain enough wriggle room to make them politically viable, while still meaningfully lowering emissions. Hashing out what NDCs should include required careful negotiation. It was decided, at a summit in Lima in 2014, that the poorest and most vulnerable countries – which contribute the least to climate change but will suffer its effects most acutely – needed to commit only to developing in a low-carbon way. All other countries, developed and developing alike, were obliged to make plans to reduce their emissions, though the mechanisms (such as increased use of renewable energy, or carbon sequestration) and speed with which they did so could vary. Countries were also encouraged, but not required, to outline measures to help the world adapt to climate change, including financial support from rich countries to poor ones.

When countries signed up to the Paris agreement, negotiated at COP21 in 2015, they committed to a common goal: keeping the world's average temperature to "well below" 2°C above pre-industrial levels, and "pursuing efforts to limit it to 1.5°C" above pre-industrial levels. They also promised to produce NDCs to show how they might get there. These laid out countries' targets for reducing emissions over a clearly articulated period, and the steps they would take to achieve their goals. Letting countries (mostly) make their own decisions on emissions meant that many more signed up than might have done under a more prescriptive accord. Big emitters such as China and India submitted themselves to scrutiny for the first time. But such flexibility also meant that no country made commitments large enough to meet the Paris agreement's goals: the first tranche of NDCs was expected to lead to global warming of around 3°C. Accordingly, the Paris agreement also outlined a "ratchet mechanism", by which countries were meant to increase the ambition and scope of their NDCs every five years.

Countries were meant to submit their updated NDCs ahead of the COP26, the UN climate summit that was scheduled to take place in Glasgow in November 2020. That plan, like so many others, was scrambled by the covid-19 pandemic, and COP26 was delayed until November 2021. In the event only a handful of countries strengthened their targets. Britain promised to reduce its greenhouse gas emissions by at least 68% by 2030, compared with 1990 levels. The 27 members of the European Union pledged to reduce their emissions by "at least 55%" across the same period. China has proposed, but not formally submitted, a new target of reaching carbon neutrality before 2060. India announced a target of net-zero emissions by 2070 but has yet to reveal detailed plans about how it will get there. Such commitments are a step in the right direction, but without more ambitious NDCs, the world will fall short of meeting the targets of the Paris agreement.

What would different levels of global warming look like?

The Paris agreement, negotiated at a United Nations summit in 2015, committed its 194 signatory countries (plus the European Union) to try to keep the world's average temperature to "well below" 2°C above pre-industrial levels, and if possible 1.5°C. The world is already perilously close to that target. In recent years, the average global temperature has regularly been at least 1°C higher than those recorded at the end of the 19th century; in 2020, it was 1.2°C more. The World Meteorological Organisation, a UN agency, predicts that there is "at least a one in five chance of it temporarily exceeding 1.5°C by 2024". Most of that warming has occurred since 1975, at a rate of about 0.15–0.2°C per decade. Accumulating greenhouse gases in the atmosphere make further warming inevitable. But what difference will a few tenths of a degree make?

1.5°C

The world is already experiencing increasingly erratic weather, including stronger storms and more unpredictable and extreme rainfall patterns, leading to deluges in some places and droughts in others. Even if global average temperature increases are stabilised at 1.5°C, they would still get worse. The annual probability of a heatwave – defined as four days with maximum temperatures above the 99th percentile of a normal warm season – in any given part of the world would rise from 5% to 28%. Sea levels would rise by 40–80cm, swelled by melting glaciers, the breakdown of Arctic ice and the expanded volume of warmer oceans. That is more than enough to drown low-lying island nations such as the Maldives. Destructive wildfires like those seen in Australia and on America's west coast in recent years will also become more frequent. For many people, these changes have already happened. More than a fifth of the world's population lives in areas where temperatures in the warmest seasons have already risen by more than 1.5°C (as an average between 2006 and 2015).

2°C

According to the Intergovernmental Panel on Climate Change (IPCC), the body tasked by the United Nations with collating the science around global warming, there is a "robust difference" between the impact of 1.5°C of warming and that of 2°C. Sea levels could rise by an additional 10cm by 2100. Higher seas pose even greater threats to small island states as well as low-lying coastal and delta areas like Bangladesh and the lands around the Nile. Periods of extreme heat will also become even more likely. Cities such as Karachi in Pakistan or Kolkata in India could face annual heatwaves like those in 2015, which killed thousands of people. More than 400m extra people could be exposed to extreme heat. Hundreds of millions more will face poverty as a result of a loss of agriculture and food insecurity. Many will be forced to migrate, alongside those displaced by rising oceans and possible increased fighting over scarce resources like food and water, says the IPCC. Not only humans will suffer. At 2°C of warming, 18% of insect species will lose more than half their habitats, as will 16% of plants and 8% of vertebrates. Almost all coral would be wiped out. (Even at 1.5°C, only 10–30% would remain.) These impacts on global biodiversity have consequences for human populations too. Insects pollinate crops. Plants soak up carbon dioxide from the atmosphere. Coral reefs are nurseries for fish populations, thereby supporting human fisheries.

Beyond 2°C

The relationship between rising temperatures and damage is not linear. Three degrees of warming above pre-industrial temperatures would not be twice as bad as 1.5°C, or half-again as 2°C. The more temperatures rise, the more the world risks passing a series of tipping points, setting off changes that will fundamentally shift how the planet behaves (though scientists are uncertain when these will occur). One abrupt change would be the breakdown of the global ocean circulation system, which helps distribute heat around the world (eg through the Gulf Stream) and determines regional weather patterns. Others include rainforests turning to savannah, collapses or shifts in monsoon patterns, the disintegration of Arctic or Antarctic ice sheets and vast amounts of methane being released by thawing permafrost.

Each scenario could play out in ways almost impossible to predict. Consequences could range from the spread of deserts to the collapse of farmable land, drastic changes in weather patterns and further temperature rise. None is good. The purpose of pledges to stabilise temperature rise at close to 1.5°C is to avoid the worst of these consequences. But despite the commitments made in the Paris agreement and in the years since, the world is still on track to exceed 2°C of warming. A seemingly small difference in degrees will have a big impact on how habitable the world remains.

Healthy interest: medical mysteries explained

Which type of plant-based milk is best?

For centuries, "milk" has been the white stuff you pour into your porridge or stir into tea or coffee. Scientifically, it refers to an aqueous solution of fat, sugars, proteins and minerals produced by mammals' mammary glands, designed to provide their young offspring with essential nutrition. Notwithstanding the pockets of humanity who preferred buffalo, camel or goat milk, milk has mostly come from cows. The ubiquity of cow's milk has had unpleasant consequences for the majority of humanity incapable of digesting it: the lactose-intolerant drink their coffee black and eat their toast dry. It has also had unpleasant consequences for the planet. Cows (raised for milk, beef and other products) are responsible for about 65% of the greenhouse gas emissions of the world's livestock. These days, however, consumers looking for an alternative are spoiled for choice. Plant-based milks are everywhere, in more than a dozen varieties. Which is best? It depends what you are looking for.

Most plant-based milks are made from nuts or seeds, which have a milk-like function – meaning that they contain, just as mothers' milk does, nutrients essential for the flourishing of the young. The precise milk-making process varies by crop and company, but it usually involves some combination of milling, grinding, soaking, filtering and adding – often sugar or flavourings or, in the case of oat milk, enzymes that turn starches into sugars. Their prominence and ubiquity may be new, but their lineage is ancient: soy milk has been consumed in China for centuries, as has rice milk in Mexico, where it is known as horchata.

Which of these is most nutritious? Cow's milk abounds in protein, potassium, calcium and B vitamins, most of which are not naturally found in non-dairy milks. But many plant milks are enriched with extra nutrients, such as calcium and vitamin D. Many also contain large amounts of added sugar. Soy milk has around the same amount of protein as cow's milk, which is more than most plant-based milks, but some worry about soy's oestrogen-mimicking compounds (frequent consumption of soy products may be linked to reduced sperm counts in men, though the evidence is thin). Although nuts themselves are high in protein, nut milks are not; the next best bet protein-wise is pea milk, though this can be relatively difficult to find. Oat milk contains fibre, though not nearly as much as oats themselves, while rice milk is almost wholly nutrition-free, and contains the sort of carbohydrates that can convert quickly into glucose.

The other major factor to consider is the environmental impact of each type of milk's production. Here too the answer is complicated, because plants can be grown responsibly or irresponsibly – though one choice is an outlier. It takes about four litres of water to produce a single almond, and most of the world's almonds are grown in drought-stricken California. Soy requires a relatively large amount of land to grow, but legumes do have a symbiotic relationship with bacteria that convert atmospheric nitrogen into a type that nourishes soil. That reduces the need for nitrogen-heavy fertilisers, which means less ocean-damaging nitrogen run-off (the same is true for peas, which are also legumes). Oats require less water than most other plants that can be turned into milk. Although oat milk is not as nutrient-rich as soy or pea milk, it beats most others on this score too.

Why sperm counts are falling across the rich world

In Stanley Kubrick's film *Dr Strangelove*, set during the cold war, an American air-force general orders a retaliatory nuclear strike against the Soviet Union. It is later revealed that the Soviets did not attack first. Instead the commander, who had a mental breakdown, ordered the strike because he had become convinced that communists had fluoridated America's water supply in an effort to damage the "precious bodily fluids" of America's men. The paranoid commander's fears about his fertility were easy to mock in 1964, when Kubrick's film was first released. But the premise may be getting closer to reality with each passing day.

In 2017, Shanna Swan of the Mount Sinai School of Medicine in New York and Hagai Levine of Hadassah-Hebrew University in Jerusalem, along with six other researchers, estimated the average sperm count for 43,000 men in 55 countries across the world. The data, from 185 previously published studies, suggest that sperm counts fell by about 25% between 1973 and 2011. But the academics performed a regression analysis that controlled for variation in the studies' sampling technique, their potential sample bias, the age of men and their level of abstinence before a sample was taken. They found that sperm counts had in fact fallen by about 50% in Western countries over the period. Although the data were less plentiful, similar trends were observed in developing countries.

Dr Swan's book, *Count Down*, published in 2021, investigates why this decline has occurred. The most likely culprit, she argues, is the proliferation of harmful chemicals such as bisphenol A (BPA) – which is most commonly found in household plastic goods. Human endocrine systems, which produce hormones including testosterone and oestrogen, can be adversely affected by these chemicals. In some cases they reduce fertility among both men and women. One study, conducted in Boston, looked at nearly 500 young men who hoped to donate sperm. It found that the share of applicants who were sufficiently fertile to donate had fallen from 69% to 44% in the ten years to 2013. But BPA chemicals may not

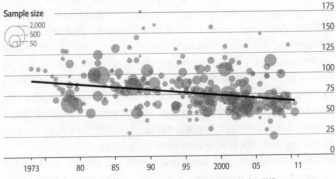

We're not going to make babies

Average sperm concentration, million per millilitre

244 estimates from 185 studies

Source: "Temporal trends in sperm count", by H. Levine et al., *Human Reproduction Update*, 2017

be solely to blame. Another study, published by *Environmental Pollution* in 2018, collected the semen samples from 5,000 men living in northern Italy between 2010 and 2016. By geocoding the men's home addresses it found that sperm counts deteriorated most in places where air pollution was highest.

Even if BPA chemicals are not the sole cause of the decline in sperm counts, regulators have been slow to catch on to the proven harm they cause. In 2007 the European Union implemented REACH (registration, evaluation, authorisation and restriction of chemicals), a set of regulations to control the import and production of hazardous chemicals. America and the EU have since banned the use of BPA in baby bottles, but the chemical is still allowed in the linings of food cans. The decline in sperm counts, were it to continue, could have dire consequences. If the rich-world trend observed by Dr Swan in her 2017 study continued until 2045, it might render half the men of Europe and North America infertile. But that seems unlikely for two reasons. The effect of BPAs on sperm may diminish as their counts decline; and already fewer BPA chemicals are being used.

What is naloxone, and how does it reverse opioid overdoses?

More than 100,000 Americans died from drug overdoses between July 2020 and June 2021, according to provisional figures released by the Centres for Disease Control and Prevention in January 2022. That is the highest number on record. Some 75% of these deaths were caused by opioids, a class of drug that includes heroin and fentanyl, a prescription painkiller that has flooded the black market. In an attempt to prevent more deaths, New York has become the first American city to open officially authorised safe-injection sites where people can inject drugs under the supervision of trained staff. They provide access to clean needles and disposal facilities, and staff can administer naloxone, a drug that rapidly reverses the effect of an opioid overdose. Within the first two months of the clinics opening in late November 2021, naloxone had reversed at least seven overdoses – each time potentially saving a life. This prompted health officials to propose the introduction of vending machines around the city that dispense the drug. What is naloxone, and how does it work?

Opioids work by attaching to receptors in nerve cells, altering the cells' activity. In particular, opioids block pain signals sent from the brain, which can cause feelings of euphoria, making them highly addictive if taken regularly. Opioids also relax a person's breathing. During an overdose a person's breathing can stop entirely, killing them. Naloxone, which is administered as an injection or nasal spray, has a stronger binding affinity with opioid receptors than the opioid itself, and so displaces the drug. The medicine causes no reaction, allowing the nerve cell to revert to its normal state. But dislodging the opioid can cause users to feel painful withdrawal symptoms if they are addicted. In the case of overdoses, naloxone allows users to breathe again, which can save their lives.

The life-saving potential of naloxone is well documented. A survey by the National Harm Reduction Coalition, a New York-based advocacy group, found that between 1996 and 2014, 136 community organisations in America gave out over 150,000 naloxone kits. They received reports of 26,463 overdose reversals, which is almost certainly an undercount. Rahul Gupta, director of America's Office of National Drug Control Policy, said in 2021 at his swearing-in that increasing naloxone's availability was his first priority. Not everyone sees expanding access to naloxone as free of problems. Some worry about a moral hazard; that it will encourage opioid users to take risks. But a review in the *International Journal of Drug Policy* looking at take-home naloxone programmes, in which the medicine is given to users and witnesses, found no evidence of increased opioid use or overdoses as a result.

Community groups are currently responsible for a large share of the drug's distribution, but it is expensive. Many of them rely solely on Pfizer, an American pharmaceutical giant, which offers a concessionary rate for a generic injectable version of the drug. Problems with Pfizer's supply chain in 2021 led to shortages and a backlog of orders. On the open market, kits cost anywhere between $30 and $75, a price at which activists say they are unable to meet demand. All states in America prescribe and distribute naloxone, but to varying degrees. At least 14 states have some provision that either enforces or recommends that naloxone is prescribed to any patient who is also taking a high-dosage opioid. The White House has proposed a model law for states that would, among other measures, make this compulsory. And although many emergency-service staff carry naloxone, they often arrive too late to save a life, not least because witnesses can be hesitant to call 911 for fear of police involvement. Getting naloxone into more people's hands would not help solve America's opioid crisis, but would save lives.

How environmental damage can lead to new diseases

The world's monitored populations of wild animals have decreased by an average of 68% in the past 50 years, according to the World Wide Fund for Nature. Deforestation, intensive farming and the changing use of land are largely to blame. But nature can recover, provided it is given a chance. COP15, a UN biodiversity summit that took place in October 2021, sought to do just that. More than 100 countries recognised the need to reverse species decline by 2030 and acknowledged the consequences of harmful environmental practices and climate change for biodiversity. These efforts are long overdue – and not just for the sake of wildlife. The same actions that threaten ecosystems also endanger human health.

Growing evidence points to a connection between destructive environmental practices and emerging diseases. Exactly how one leads to the other is not yet fully understood, as the struggle to establish the origin of covid-19 shows (the virus may have leaked from a lab, but seems more likely to have "spilled over" from bats into humans, via an intermediary species). Why are changes in ecosystems linked to the spread of disease, and what increases the risk of outbreaks?

Of more than 330 diseases which emerged between 1940 and 2004, nearly two-thirds were zoonotic, meaning they were transmitted from animals to humans, as happened with HIV/AIDS and (probably) covid-19. Of those over 70% originated in wildlife, as opposed to domesticated animals. And although many factors are involved in disease transmission, including population growth, migration and climate change, scientists are increasingly turning their attention to how changes in land use interfere with a pathogen's journey from animals to humans. A study published in March 2021 by researchers at Montpellier University and Aix-Marseille University found a link between changes in global forest cover between 1990 and 2016 and an increase in reported epidemics, even accounting for the fact that deforestation usually means more humans living nearby. As forest cover shrank (from 31.6% to 30.7%), occurrences of diseases rose, particularly in tropical, biodiverse areas.

One likely reason for the increase in pathogens is that felling trees increases contact between humans and disease-carrying animals. Scientists found a correlation between the loss of forests in west and central Africa and outbreaks of Ebola between 2004 and 2014. The Ebola virus is thought to be transmitted by infected bats and primates, although exactly how is not yet fully understood. And interactions with other mammals are not the only concern. Cutting down trees may also increase the threat to humans posed by viral infections transmitted through mosquito bites, such as Zika, dengue and chikungunya. Researchers at the University of Florida analysed studies of 87 mosquito species in 12 countries. About half of the species were associated with deforested environments. Of these, more than half are known to carry diseases.

Replacing old-growth forests with a single crop, such as oil palm, can also increase the transmission of disease. If predators' habitats are destroyed and their populations dwindle, other creatures such as rodents, mosquitoes, bats and some primates can proliferate. These harbour potentially zoonotic pathogens and tend to cluster in places where they will be more frequently exposed to humans and livestock. Rodents, for example, often inhabit the border areas between newly created pastures and forests. A study published in 2020 by disease ecologists in *Science* described the edges of tropical forests as "a major launch-pad" for new viruses. Wildlife may also move towards human settlements in search of food. Mango trees planted on pig farms in Malaysia probably attracted fruit bats carrying nipah, a virus that infected local pig farmers in 1999 and still breaks out yearly in Bangladesh.

Ultimately, more work is needed to understand how people's interactions with nature spread disease. But the emergence of new pathogens, such as the virus that causes covid-19, has given efforts to preserve the planet's biodiversity a new importance.

How bad are e-cigarettes for you?

The regulators at America's Food and Drug Administration could be forgiven for wanting a cigarette break. They rushed to meet a September 2021 deadline to decide whether more than 6.5m e-cigarette products made by over 500 companies could remain on the market. When the deadline arrived, the agency had made determinations covering about 93% of the products submitted for review. It said it would block the sale of more than 946,000 flavoured products. But on the question of Juul – the largest player, with 40% of the market for e-cigarettes – regulators said they needed more time. E-cigarettes have attracted keen government attention in recent years. In 2019 America's surgeon general called vaping an epidemic among young people, criticising in particular products with "kid-friendly" flavours, such as cinnamon and vanilla. Later that year more than 450 people in America suffered from a mysterious and severe lung illness that was linked to vaping, and was probably caused by black-market cartridges containing cannabis extracts and harmful substances such as vitamin E oil. Other countries, including Brazil, India and Singapore, have banned e-cigarettes altogether. So what goes into e-cigarettes, and how bad are they really?

The devices use an electric charge to vaporise a dose of nicotine (often accompanied by various flavouring chemicals). The composition of the vapour varies between brands. Its main ingredients – propylene glycol and glycerol – are thought to be mostly harmless when inhaled. But that is not certain. Nitrosamines, a carcinogenic family of chemicals, have been found in e-cigarette vapour, albeit at levels low enough to be deemed insignificant. Metallic particles from the device's heating element, such as nickel and cadmium, are also a concern. High exposure to these can increase the risk of cancer. And some studies have found that the vapour can contain high levels of unambiguously nasty chemicals such as formaldehyde, acetaldehyde and acrolein, all derived from other ingredients that have been exposed to high temperatures. It also contains free radicals, highly oxidising substances that can damage tissue or DNA, and which are thought to come mostly from flavourings. Then there is nicotine. Besides being addictive, it is known to have adverse effects all around the body. The main concern is its effects on children. Work in animals suggests that exposure to nicotine at an early age could make users more susceptible to other addictive substances later in life.

All this sounds worrying, but e-cigarettes are nowhere near as nasty as their combustible cousins. Cigarette smoke contains about 70 carcinogens, as well as carbon monoxide (a poison), particulates, toxic heavy metals such as cadmium and arsenic, oxidising chemicals and assorted other organic compounds. Instead of the thousands of different compounds in cigarette smoke, e-cigarette vapour probably contains merely hundreds. And cigarettes may be more addictive than some e-cigarettes because they deliver other chemicals along with nicotine. For example, tobacco smoke amplifies the addictive nature of nicotine by inhibiting monoamine oxidase, an enzyme that helps to break down the dopamine (a pleasure hormone) that nicotine releases in the brain.

Regulators and politicians are right to worry about the long-term effects of e-cigarettes, but widespread bans risk forgoing the potential health benefits that ensue when people turn to e-cigarettes as a substitute for the conventional sort. And the tide may be turning on the vaping epidemic among teenagers. The proportion of America's high-school students vaping fell from 27.5% in 2019 to 19.6% in 2021, according to the National Youth Tobacco Survey. But smoking still kills 480,000 Americans every year, and 8m people worldwide. That means regulators must strike a fine balance: helping existing smokers to quit while deterring a new generation of nicotine addicts. E-cigarettes are not good for you, but they are better than smoking.

What are DNA vaccines?

India hopes that a new approach to vaccination will give it a better shot at tackling covid-19. In August 2021 the country's drug regulator granted emergency-use approval for ZyCoV-D – the world's first DNA vaccine to be authorised for humans. Zydus Cadila, the vaccine's developer, said it planned to make up to 120m doses annually. DNA vaccines could play a part in fighting other illnesses such as cancer and HIV too. So how do they work, and do they differ from other vaccines already in use?

Conventional vaccines work by turning a virus against itself. A significantly weakened or inactivated form of the virus is injected into the body, training the immune system to act rapidly against the live virus, should it appear. But growing large amounts of a virus and weakening or extracting parts of it can be fiddly and laborious, especially if the target virus keeps mutating. Starting in the late 20th century, scientists therefore tried to devise a simpler way of teaching the body to fight off an illness. This led to a new form of immunisation: genetic vaccines.

Some vaccines being used against covid-19, notably those developed by Pfizer/BioNTech and Moderna, are based on messenger ribonucleic acid (mRNA). This is a molecule that normally carries instructions to make a particular protein from a cell's DNA, in the nucleus, to the cell's molecular factories. Introducing mRNA into the body in the form of vaccine in effect presses the body's own cells into service as drug factories. The cells follow the mRNA's instructions and produce proteins (in the case of covid-19, the spike proteins found on the virus's outer coating) that prime the immune system. DNA vaccines, such as ZyCoV-D, begin one step back in the process. Developers start with DNA that describes the spike protein, and deliver it into the cell. This DNA is then transcribed into mRNA, which in turn instructs the cell to make the relevant protein, priming the immune system.

Both DNA and mRNA vaccines have robust safety records and far lower production costs than conventional vaccines. They can also be easily adapted to deal with mutations of the virus. But DNA vaccines have an advantage over their mRNA counterparts: they are more convenient to transport and store, making them much easier to distribute in poor countries with weak infrastructure. ZyCoV-D is stored between 2°C and 8°C but has shown good stability at temperatures of 25°C for at least three months. Pfizer's mRNA-based vaccine, however, is stored at temperatures as low as −80°C. Results from a phase III clinical trial in India, published in the *Lancet*, a medical journal, in April 2022, showed the ZyCoV-D vaccine was 66.6% effective at preventing symptomatic cases. That is lower than some other covid-19 vaccines, such as Pfizer's, but still offers useful protection.

DNA vaccines have unlocked yet another new kind of vaccination to experiment with in the fight against covid-19 and other illnesses. More could soon come to market. Inovio, an American biotech company, has its own vaccine in late-stage trials, as does Osaka University with AnGes and Takara Bio, two Japanese companies. And genetic vaccines are being touted as potential treatments for other illnesses such as cancer, where the vaccines would turbocharge the immune system by delivering genetic information that teaches it to recognise tumour antigens. The pandemic has fast-tracked these innovative methods of vaccination. Their funding could now have implications for other diseases, long after covid-19 ceases to be a grave threat.

Why are coronavirus variants named using the Greek alphabet?

Alpha, beta, gamma, delta. Those affected by covid-19 – which is, one way or another, more or less everyone on the planet – have become more familiar with the ancient Greek alphabet after the World Health Organisation (WHO) introduced, in May 2021, a new way to refer to variants of concern of SARS-CoV-2, the virus that causes the illness. There are two reasons for this new nomenclature: simplicity and the avoidance of hurt feelings.

The simplicity is obvious. The variant now known as Beta, for example, was the second to be designated a variant of concern, and had previously been known as 501Y.V2, B.1.351, 20H/501Y.V2, GH/501Y.V2 or "the South African variant", depending on whom you asked. Those old names have not been abandoned. Experts continue to use such names when referring to specific variants, subvariants and their offshoots. But for general purposes, the simplicity of "Beta" is probably better – as is "Alpha" for B.1.1.7, etc, the so-called Kent or British variant, "Gamma" for P.1, etc (the Brazilian variant), "Delta" for B.1.617.2 (the Indian variant) and "Omicron" for B.1.1.529. The Greek-letter names are generally capitalised when used to refer to viral variants.

As for the desire to avoid hurt feelings, some may consider it oversensitivity. As the list above suggests, it is common, if not always official practice, to refer to viruses by the name of the place where they were first identified. The Ebola virus is named after a river in Congo, the Zika virus after a forest in Uganda and the West Nile virus after a district of that country. Similarly, the influenza pandemic of 1968 was widely known at the time as "Hong Kong" flu, even though it almost certainly originated in mainland China. That was a lot simpler for the public than calling it H3N2, after the particular versions of two proteins, haemagglutinin and neuraminidase, that characterised it. Likewise, the H2N2 outbreak of 1957, first detected in Singapore, was known in the West as Asian flu.

Whether the people of Kent felt tarnished by the fact that SARS-CoV-2 variant now known as Alpha was first detected in their part of England is moot. Some Spaniards, though, certainly are miffed that the influenza pandemic of 1918 to 1920 was widely known as Spanish flu even though it did not originate in Spain. In that case the reason was that the countries where the illness was rife early in its history were at war, and wartime censorship played the epidemic down. The press in neutral Spain was not so constrained and reported on the outbreak in detail, resulting in the misunderstanding. More recently, in the context of the covid-19 pandemic, some people, including Donald Trump, took to referring to SARS-CoV-2 as "the Chinese virus" in a way that many felt went beyond mere neutral labelling, and shaded into propaganda and name-calling.

Hence the Greek-letter labelling introduced by the WHO, which provides the convenience of simple, uncontroversial monikers. Greek letters are often used as parts of scientific labels, which adds authority to the idea. And, at least to those familiar with the alphabet concerned, the names instantly convey information about what order the variants were discovered in. As far as the virus itself is concerned, of course, none of this matters one iota.

How did China eradicate malaria?

Malaria has afflicted humans for thousands of years and has killed people on every continent except Antarctica. It was not until 1880, when Alphonse Laveran, a French military surgeon, performed autopsies on malaria victims, that scientists realised the illness was caused by parasites. Ronald Ross, a British doctor, discovered that these parasites were transmitted via mosquitoes in 1897. In the 20th century alone as many as 300m people may have died of the disease – a chilling 5% of all deaths. In 2019, 87 countries reported a total of 229m malaria cases, yet the illness has been eradicated in many places. On June 30th 2021 China was certified "malaria-free" by the World Health Organisation (WHO), a status granted to countries that have seen no transmission of the disease for "at least the previous three consecutive years".

In 2016 the WHO identified 21 countries that could eliminate malaria by 2020: of those, Algeria, China, El Salvador and Paraguay now seem to have succeeded. Iran, Malaysia and Timor-Leste have had two consecutive years of no cases. Other countries have had more trouble eradicating the scourge. Cases of malaria in South Africa surged from 8,060 in 2010 to 23,381 in 2017 – which may have been the result of a particularly severe monsoon season, as standing water encourages mosquito breeding – before decreasing to 3,096 in 2019. Costa Rica appeared to have eradicated the disease between 2013 and 2015, but has since seen infections rise steeply. Since 2018 the Costa Rican Ministry of Health has increased monitoring of agricultural sites, such as banana plantations, which offer prime conditions for malaria-carrying mosquitoes.

How did China manage it? In the 1940s China had an estimated 30m indigenous cases (ie the infection was locally contracted) and 300,000 deaths a year. As recently as 2010 it recorded nearly 5,000 cases, but that figure dropped to zero in 2017. China's achievement is a result of three policies: early intervention, surveillance and cross-sector collaboration. In 1955 Chinese authorities launched the National Malaria Control Programme, which promoted the

Buzz off

Number of indigenous malaria cases in selected E-2020 countries,* '000

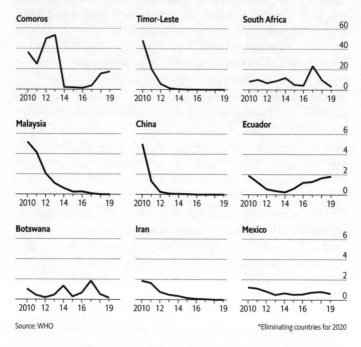

Source: WHO

*Eliminating countries for 2020

use of insecticide sprays, improved irrigation and case detection, and increased the provision of anti-malarial treatments. Though simple, these measures helped achieve steady progress in the country. By 1990 mortality rates had declined by 95%.

In 2010 the Chinese Ministry of Health brought together 13 government departments to implement the Malaria Elimination Action Plan, an ambitious scheme to eliminate malaria by 2020. Its success mainly relied on the "1-3-7" strategy. First, health facilities must report any suspected malaria cases within a day. Second, authorities have three days to confirm and investigate the cases. Last, appropriate action to stop further spread, such as spraying the walls and other surfaces of a house with a residual insecticide, must be taken within seven days.

When the covid-19 pandemic hit, the Chinese government continued to monitor at-risk zones. Online training for health providers remained available and virtual meetings were held to discuss patient treatment. Other countries, however, have had to divert resources usually reserved for malaria to deal with the coronavirus. The WHO estimates that covid-19 disrupted about a third of countries' efforts to prevent, diagnose and treat malaria in the first three months of 2021. Neglecting malaria in favour of covid-19 may mean that hard-won progress has been undone. Between 2000 and 2019 the number of deaths attributed to malaria fell by 60%. But an estimate published in the *Lancet*, a medical journal, suggests that interruptions to malaria-control programmes could lead to an increase in malaria-related deaths of as much as 36% in the next five years.

Follow the money: assessing assets, old and new

Why Tel Aviv is the world's most expensive city

The city of Tel Aviv was named after the title in Hebrew of "Old-New Land" (*Altneuland* in German), a visionary novel published in 1902 by Theodor Herzl, the founder of modern Zionism. Israel's commercial capital still blends modernity and history. In the summer of 2021, as busy professionals were ordering coffee pods delivered by drone, archaeologists nearby were uncovering a Byzantine wine press and a 7th-century gold coin. Both discoveries might come in handy in the city that is now the world's most expensive.

According to the latest findings of the Worldwide Cost of Living Survey from The Economist Intelligence Unit (EIU), our sister company, a strong shekel and rising prices for alcohol, groceries and transport have pushed Tel Aviv to the top of the ranking, up four places from 2020. Paris, which shared the top spot with Hong Kong and Zurich that year, is now the second-priciest place to live, alongside Singapore. The survey, which compares the prices of more than 200 products and services in 173 cities around the world, is primarily used by firms to negotiate appropriate compensation when relocating staff, but it can also reveal pricing trends at both the local and global levels.

Supply-chain problems related to the pandemic pushed the price of goods up in much of the world. In September 2021 the cost of shipping a standard container was four times higher than a year earlier. Some cities experienced additional pressure. American sanctions imposed on Iran pushed its capital, Tehran, 50 places up the ranking to 29th. The price of the EIU's basket of goods and services there rose by 42% in local-currency terms compared with November 2020. But this was dwarfed by a 1,766% increase in Caracas, thanks in part to price controls imposed by Venezuela's government. Even excluding a handful of such cities with very high inflation, the EIU's data show average global prices rose by 3.5% year-on-year in local-currency terms, compared with just 1.9% in 2020.

Growing apart

City cost of living index, September 2021
New York=100

Ten most expensive cities

1	Tel Aviv	106
2=	Paris	104
2=	Singapore	104
4	Zurich	103
5	Hong Kong	101
6	*New York*	*100*
7	Geneva	99
8	Copenhagen	97
9	Los Angeles	96
10	Osaka	94

Source: The Economist Intelligence Unit

Prices did not rise everywhere. Rome saw the biggest drop, falling 16 places to 48th, with a particularly sharp decline in the clothing category as even fashionable Italians gave up dressing up for the home office. And most American cities fell in the rankings, thanks to government stimulus injected into the economy during the pandemic. (New York remains the costliest American city, in sixth place.) But the general picture is one of disruption and higher prices. When the survey was undertaken, in August and September 2021, the average cost of a litre of unleaded petrol across all cities was 21% higher than a year before. Since then, oil and gas prices have surged, driven by energy shortages in late 2021 and by Russia's invasion of Ukraine in February 2022. The war in Ukraine has also pushed up the price of food and other commodities (both Russia and Ukraine are usually large exporters of grain). As a result the cost of living has increased for almost everyone in 2022.

Which countries have decoupled GDP growth from emissions?

Every year, carbon dioxide (CO_2) is pumped into the atmosphere from dirty combustion and power plants. Over the past two centuries, more than 1trn tonnes of greenhouse gases have caused the Earth's temperature to rise. Dramatic reductions in emissions are needed to limit global warming. It looks at last as though this might be happening. A recent report from the Global Carbon Project, a research organisation, found that over the past decade global CO_2 emissions have started to reach a plateau.

Though many poorer countries such as China and India have increased their carbon emissions in the past ten years, this has been roughly balanced by reductions in emissions from America and much of Europe. In total 76 countries have reduced their CO_2 output per person by more than 5% since 2010. During the 2010s these countries collectively reduced their yearly carbon emissions by about 1.4 gigatonnes, more than the CO_2 output of the whole of Africa in 2019.

Although increasing emissions have historically gone hand-in-hand with economic growth, several rich countries are now bucking this trend. In two dozen countries, including America, Britain and France, GDP per person has increased since 2010 while carbon emissions have fallen. This has not come about merely through a shift of production – and hence pollution – to other countries. Most of the countries that experienced GDP growth along with a decline in CO_2 emissions also decreased their average citizen's consumption of CO_2, which takes into account pollutants produced at home, plus any trade emissions – those associated with a country's imports of goods and services, minus the CO_2 produced from exports. Some countries, such as America, Denmark and Switzerland, did have a slight increase in their net trade emissions per person, but this was drastically outweighed by reductions at home.

Still, there is a long way to go if the world is to prevent catastrophic global warming. Even if emissions in these 24 emission-reducing

Growing apart

Selected countries, GDP growth and CO_2 emissions reductions

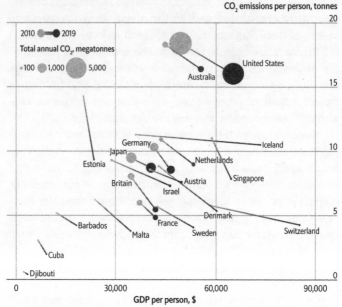

CO_2 emissions per person, tonnes

Sources: Our World in Data; World Bank

countries continue to fall at the same rate, it would take more than 80 years for them to reach zero. The trend may be that emissions are falling, but they are not falling fast enough.

Can bitcoin be bettered?

Regulators around the world have been cracking down on cryptocurrencies in general, and bitcoin in particular. In June 2021 China ordered several state-owned banks and Alipay, a fintech giant, to track and block transactions linked to it. Among other things, regulators worry about the environmental damage caused by the mechanism that bitcoin uses to verify transactions and put new coins into circulation, known as "proof of work" (POW). In periods of high activity, the computers in the bitcoin network burn more energy than the whole of Argentina. The glaring inefficiencies of that process also explain why payments in bitcoin are slow and costly, thus inhibiting its use as an actual currency. That has fed appetite for alternative verification mechanisms, the most popular of which is dubbed "proof of stake" (POS). Ether, the second-most-popular cryptocurrency after bitcoin, is preparing to switch to it; some smaller coins already use it. What is POS, and can it solve bitcoin's problems?

The rationale for POW is tied up with that of bitcoin itself. As a decentralised currency, bitcoin lacks a trusted central authority that validates transactions. Instead it relies on a public consensus mechanism where each block of transactions is validated by someone on the network and then verified by everyone else – a process known as mining. Miners put blocks together by picking pending transactions from a pool, ascertaining they are legitimate by checking, for example, that bitcoins are being spent by their true owner. To earn the right to add their block to the blockchain – the distributed database that records transactions – miners compete to solve a complex numerical problem using super-fast computers. The one who does so first is rewarded in new bitcoins (hence the term "mining", because the verification of each new block results in the creation of new coins). This whole process sucks up huge amounts of energy, making POW both an ecological disaster and a crummy verification method (bitcoin can only process around seven transactions per second).

POS is an alternative consensus mechanism which doles out rewards based not on who first solves a mathematical puzzle, but how much has been "staked" by competing validators. To earn the chance to validate transactions, network users must place coins in a specific digital wallet, where that sum – the stake – will remain frozen until the block of transactions is processed. Instead of favouring those with the most computing power, POS picks winners at random, with the probability of being chosen linked to the amount staked. Unlike POW, which pays miners with both a reward every time they create a new block and a fee per transaction, POS does only the latter. All this means the process requires far less equipment and energy than POW. Validators are incentivised to keep the network secure: the more they stake, the more they earn, but the more they also stand to lose if they try to hack the network or validate fraudulent transactions.

That said, POS has downsides too. It is less effective at putting new currency into circulation. It also encourages hoarding, since the probability of earning big fees rises in tandem with how much is held in escrow wallets, rather than spent in transactions. That is bad for a currency's availability and liquidity, which limits its usefulness and makes its value more volatile. It could also end up concentrating verification powers in fewer and fewer hands, defeating the purpose of decentralisation. In POW, by contrast, miners are encouraged not to cling on to their crypto, because to engage in the mining arms race they constantly need fresh real-world funds to upgrade their hardware. This unsatisfactory state of affairs has led to a mushrooming of hybrid protocols, such as "proof of activity" or "proof of burn". Others, such as "proof of capacity", which rewards users based on how much space they have on their hard drives, use different methods. But none of them has yet managed to steal POW's crown and knock bitcoin off the top spot.

What are stablecoins, such as Tether?

Although 86% of Americans have heard of cryptocurrencies, only 16% have traded or paid with them according to the Pew Research Centre, a think-tank. One reason for that gap is volatility: bitcoin, the world's most popular cryptocurrency, has seesawed in value over the past decade. Stablecoins, a burgeoning class of digital currency, could help crypto to go mainstream. Many people use them as a bridge into the broader cryptosphere – the total amount issued grew from $5bn at the start of 2020 to almost $160bn by December 2021. What are these stablecoins, and how do they work?

Stablecoins are so named because they are pegged to a fixed quantity of another asset, such as the dollar. This means their prices should barely fluctuate. There are two main ways in which they are backed. In one category are coins – for instance, Tether – that claim to be fully backed by liquid assets such as cash or safe bonds stored in banks. Most exist on a public blockchain, but some exist on a private network, with the issuer controlling their use. In the second category are stablecoins backed by other cryptocurrencies. Dai, a stablecoin that can be borrowed in exchange for other cryptocurrencies, maintains a one-for-one peg with the dollar by moving a pair of interest rates, one paid by those who have borrowed the currency and one paid to those who have purchased the borrowed coins on a crypto exchange. Token-owners in Dai's governance organisation, MakerDAO, vote on the interest rate to maintain the peg and to fine-tune supply and demand.

For users to trust that a stablecoin will not budge, they need to know that its collateral is verifiable, liquid and of high quality. No coin currently has all three, says Christian Catalini, director of the Massachusetts Institute of Technology's cryptoeconomics lab. That means they could face something akin to a bank run during times of stress. If many people sell their coins at once, the issuer could be forced into a fire-sale of assets, causing the value of any remaining reserves held in unsafe assets to fall. A crisis of confidence in crypto-backed stablecoins, meanwhile, can break their pegs. In May

2022 the value of Terra, a well-known stablecoin, collapsed almost to zero when investors lost confidence in the cryptocurrency backing it, called Luna. This triggered a broader sell-off across crypto markets and caused Tether to dip briefly below its par value of $1. Regulators have taken notice. In October 2021, Tether was fined $41m for not holding enough reserves in quality assets. In America, the President's Working Group on Financial Markets has said that stablecoin issuers should be regulated as banks.

Adequately backed stablecoins could offer certain advantages over fiat currencies, however. They can be more efficient, cutting out middlemen, such as clearinghouses, in payments. Most American banks charge between $15 and $50 for wire transfers. Globally, the average cost of a $200 remittance is about 7%. Blockchain-based transfers claim to charge less than half that. But traditional banking is muscling in on these advantages. In Europe, open-banking rules have enabled cheap, fast payments across banking networks. Central-bank digital currencies, a kind of digital coin issued by central banks, hold similar promise and a growing number of governments are considering them. The lasting benefit of stablecoins, therefore, could be in connecting investors to other parts of the cryptosphere. Those who want to buy digital assets such as NFTs (non-fungible tokens – see page 166), or trade other cryptocurrencies, will use stablecoins as a safe way in. They just aren't safe enough yet.

Why are cryptocurrency prices so volatile?

The price of bitcoin, the world's most popular cryptocurrency, has fluctuated wildly in recent months. In July 2021 the price dipped below $30,000, before rising above $50,000 in September, and hitting a new high above $65,000 in November. It then declined in early 2022, falling back below $30,000 in May. Other popular coins based on rival blockchains, such as Ethereum, also experienced wild variations in value. What makes cryptocurrencies so volatile?

Though cryptocurrencies are billed as digital currencies, their holders treat them not as means of payment but as financial assets. Most are thinly traded in comparison with shares, with a few big investors holding significant sway. About 2% of bitcoin accounts hold 95% of the available coins, according to crypto-analytics firm Flipside. During 2020 less than 20% of bitcoin supply was actively traded – most is held in long-term accounts. That means trades do not have to be very large to shift prices dramatically. Crypto exchanges are numerous: the fragmentation of trading also increases volatility, as a few trades on a given exchange can have a significant effect. Prices are also affected by a massive market for derivatives (contracts based on the price of an underlying asset, in this case a cryptocurrency): there are on average five times more bitcoin derivative trades than spot trades of the coin itself. These bets, which are usually made on unregulated offshore exchanges, can shift the price of cryptocurrencies, adding to volatility.

As crypto investing gains traction, more established investors are dipping their toes into the market. That might inject more professionalism and make prices less volatile in the long term. But stability is still some way off. More regulation of crypto is likely, with different countries tightening up in different ways. America is mulling regulation for stablecoins, a type of cryptocurrency that is pegged to a government-issued currency; the European Central Bank has approved a framework for oversight of digital payments, including some cryptocurrencies. And changing expectations about interest rates may well continue to shift prices. Investing in crypto looks likely to remain a bumpy ride.

What is an NFT?

"Non-fungible tokens" (NFTs) leapt from the more obscure corners of the internet into the mainstream in March 2021 when Christies, a British auction house, sold a digital work of art for $69m. What it actually flogged was an NFT, a cryptocurrency chit that proves a buyer owns an intangible marker connected to a unique piece of digital art, music or other item. Much like René Magritte's painting of a pipe that proclaims "this is not a pipe", an NFT is not the thing it represents but is more akin to a title deed. Tweets, videos of basketball dunks and even the source code to the world wide web have been sold as NFTs. From June to September 2021 they generated almost $11bn in sales, an eight-fold increase on the previous four months, according to market tracker DappRadar. What exactly is an NFT? And why are people spending tens of millions of dollars on them?

An NFT is a record on a cryptocurrency's blockchain (an immutable ledger that can record more than just virtual coins) that represents an item of digital media. Invented a few years ago, it can link not only to art but also to text, videos or bits of code. Promoters of NFTs claim that they solve a thorny problem with digital art: how to own an original. For creators who freely upload their work or sell it as identical copies, the concept of an original is difficult to pin down. Exclusivity is impossible to enforce when digital files can be copied and shared freely on the internet. But collectors want the cachet that comes with having an exclusive claim on an artwork. This is where NFTs come in.

To mint an NFT, the creator establishes a unique record of the artwork, generally on a website. Then the creator places the record on a blockchain, usually the Ethereum blockchain, which requires paying a transaction fee known as gas. Possession of a private encryption key associated with the transaction proves ownership. This gives an artist or collector something to sell. An NFT may link to a version of the work, but rarely includes the rights to reproduce or distribute it. That differentiates it from a commercial licensing arrangement too.

NFTs have myriad problems. They are bought and sold using cryptocurrencies, the values of which are wildly volatile. The prices of NFTs, and the volume of transactions, dropped in early 2022 as part of a broader crypto sell-off. Anyone can mint an NFT, because the systems involved are decentralised, although doing so with someone else's work could infringe their copyright. Some artists have already claimed misappropriation of their work. Most NFTs are simply links to images. Unless they have been issued in a certain way to ensure they are tamper-proof, these can in theory be meddled with after the sale. The high electricity usage of blockchains has prompted arguments over whether artists are contributing to climate change by embracing NFTs. And ownership may be difficult to prove in the long term, as web-based records may not last for ever. Yet NFTs may have some value beyond the cryptocurrency hype: artists struggle to make a living when their works can be easily replicated and pirated. So far, however, it is unclear whether NFTs create more problems than they solve.

What are DAOs, or decentralised autonomous organisations?

SpiceDAO, a group of crypto investors, was ridiculed for spending $3m on a 1970s sci-fi curio. In late 2021 the group bought a rare book written by Alejandro Jodorowsky, a film-maker, containing his plans for *Dune*, an intergalactic epic that he never made (a subsequent adaptation was one of the biggest blockbusters of 2021). SpiceDAO said it intended to create an animated series based on the work. Critics sneered that the "cryptobros" had wasted their money, misunderstood copyright laws and had no right to adapt the book. But for most people the most baffling element of this story is not why a DAO, or "decentralised autonomous organisation", bought an old book. It is: what on earth is a DAO in the first place?

Bitcoin and Ethereum, the two leading cryptocurrencies, are not companies. They do not have chief executives to manage them or board members to oversee their running. Instead they are managed by consensus. The "miners" who do the work of maintaining the distributed ledgers, or blockchains, that support Ethereum or bitcoin, in effect vote on changes to how the network works by agreeing among themselves to alter the way they do things, typically with an update to their software. Getting consensus can take a long time, and developers do not always agree. If they cannot, the network "forks": one group carries on with one version of the software and the ledger, and the rest with another. Bitcoin has forked several times, creating alternative currencies called "bitcoin gold" and "bitcoin cash".

In the years since bitcoin was created, the complexity of the tasks that developers are trying to do on blockchains has grown. Bitcoin is just a ledger keeping track of ownership and movements in holdings. More modern blockchains, such as Ethereum, host applications that carry out the functions of banks or exchanges, collectively known as "decentralised finance" or "DeFi" apps. With complexity comes a need for a nimbler method of organising consensus on how software should be developed. Enter DAOs

– collectives that use automation and crowdsourcing to make decisions. They do not rely on a single central authority, such as a chief executive. Instead members typically use cryptocurrency to buy tokens, granting them voting rights. Jonah Erlich, a member of ConstitutionDAO, which tried to buy one of the original copies of the US Constitution at auction, has likened a DAO to a group chat with a bank account. They use "smart contracts", rules encoded in programs that execute themselves automatically under certain conditions, to carry out their business. Funds are only transferred, for example, if the majority of token-holders have digitally signed off on a transaction.

The first DAO to be known as such was created in 2016 by users on the Ethereum blockchain. It was intended to work like a venture-capital fund, allowing users to invest using cryptocurrency, pitch projects and potentially receive money, following a vote by its members. It quickly raised the equivalent of nearly $150m to invest in start-ups. But things quickly turned sour. Barely two months after it launched, a hacker took advantage of a loophole in the code to steal 3.6m ether, then worth around $70m. That early mishap has not stopped DAOs from proliferating. Some DAOs control stablecoins, such as dai, which is pegged to the dollar and run by MakerDAO. Token-owners vote on how the mechanisms to vary interest rates work. These maintain the peg and fine-tune supply and demand. Other DAOs speculate on cryptocurrencies and non-fungible tokens (NFTs). In December 2021 Andreessen Horowitz, a big Silicon Valley venture-capital firm, invested in PleasrDAO, which buys NFTs.

Given the sell-off across crypto markets in early 2022, it is tempting to dismiss DAOs as mechanisms that simply manage bets in a vast online casino. But DAOs are also fascinating experiments in new approaches to the democratic governance of entities which oversee billions of dollars in trading and lending. That, at least, makes them worth keeping an eye on.

How does an ancient Inca highway still benefit people today?

Spain's conquest of the Inca empire in the 16th century was catastrophic for the Incas. Within four decades the native population had fallen by 75–90%. Old-world diseases were mostly to blame, but forced labour played a part. Missionaries coerced Spain's new subjects to convert to Catholicism, while viceroys razed Inca buildings. Yet Inca culture proved resilient. Some 10m people in Peru and nearby countries speak Quechua, the Incas' language of empire, whose use the Spaniards discouraged. Peruvians still hand-weave textiles with bright patterns. And a paper by Ana Paula Franco of the University of Michigan, Sebastian Galiani of the University of Maryland and Pablo Lavado of the University of the Pacific in Lima unearths another example of the Incas' durable achievements: Peruvians still benefit from 15th-century infrastructure.

The Incas ruled over 10m square km (3.8m square miles). To collect taxes, deploy troops and exchange messages with remote lands, they built 30,000km of stone roads, dotted with warehouses to store food and water. The biggest cities in modern Peru are on or near the coast, far from the Incas' most important routes. This makes it possible to study the effects of pre-Columbian infrastructure with little distortion from later urbanisation.

To test if the Inca road, the Incas' main thoroughfare, has boosted modern living standards, the authors split the map into small squares. For four indicators of welfare – wages, nutrition, maths-test scores and years of schooling – they compared levels from 2007 to 2017 in squares crossed by the road with those in neighbouring squares not on its route. On every measure, residents of roadside squares fared better than those in adjacent ones, even after controlling for differences in such factors as the slope of terrain and the presence of rivers. Women gained more than men.

How did the road grant such long-lived blessings? The Spaniards used it to ship silver and turned the warehouses into profitmaking shops, often staffed by women (possibly inculcating more equal

Old town road

Living standards on the Incas' main road

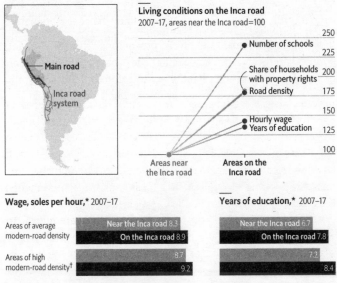

Living conditions on the Inca road
2007–17, areas near the Inca road=100

Number of schools
Share of households with property rights
Road density
Hourly wage
Years of education

Areas near the Inca road

Areas on the Inca road

Wage, soles per hour,* 2007–17

Areas of average modern-road density
Near the Inca road 8.3
On the Inca road 8.9

Areas of high modern-road density†
8.7
9.2

Years of education,* 2007–17

Near the Inca road 6.7
On the Inca road 7.8

7.2
8.4

*Modelled estimate to isolate the impact of the Inca road, adjusting for all other factors
†One standard deviation above average
Source: "Long-term effects of the Inca road", by A. P. Franco, S. Galiani
and P. Lavado, National Bureau of Economic Research, 2021

gender roles). This made land near the road unusually valuable, encouraging colonisers to settle there. The authors argue that Spaniards who moved in claimed legal title to their landholdings and built schools and new roads in the vicinity, creating enduring property rights and public goods. Today, the presence of the Inca road alone accounts for a third of the observed difference in levels of formal land ownership between dwellers on the road and those in nearby areas. It explains half the difference in the number of schools.

Might modern roads along the corridor explain more of that uplift in welfare than the ancient one? The scholars investigated that too. The Inca-road squares do have twice as many kilometres of road as adjacent ones. However, on average, even when comparing squares with similar densities of road, people living in those along the old route earned more money and had more years of schooling.

The builders of the Inca road might be pleased that the areas they improved remain relatively prosperous (though they are poorer than the coast). They would be less happy that one reason is the usefulness of their handiwork to colonisers. But today, the Incas' descendants are also among the beneficiaries of their labour.

It's all geek to me: science and technology decoded

Why do Brood X cicadas have such a strange life cycle?

Having spent months sheltering from covid-19, New Yorkers began to emerge again in May 2021. The subway resumed running 24 hours a day, and restaurants were allowed to reopen at full capacity. But humans were not the only creatures surging onto American streets after a long time hidden away. A combination of suitable weather and soil temperature prompted billions of cicadas, known as Brood X, to begin swarming in large parts of the eastern United States. The insects had last emerged in 2004. Why do these cicadas have such an unusual life cycle?

Brood X emerges around the same time of year every 17 years, and is the largest of a number of broods of periodical cicadas. Others emerge at intervals of 13 years. During that time cicada nymphs remain underground, feeding on sap from tree roots until their biological alarm clocks go off. When that happens they mature, emerge, mate, lay eggs (if female) and then die – all in four to six weeks. Climate change may be causing them to emerge earlier in the year, however, as spring temperatures rise. Gene Kritsky, a biologist at Mount St Joseph University in Cincinnati, has observed that the typical arrival of Brood X has moved from late May in the first half of the 20th century to the first two weeks of May.

Biologists believe that the strange lifestyle of periodical cicadas is an example of a survival strategy called "predator satiation". The insects emerge in such prodigious quantities that predators, such as birds and rodents, cannot possibly eat them all. Emerging every 17 years (a prime number) may also help cicadas avoid damaging "resonances" with the two- and three-year population fluctuations of their predators. An abundance of prey allows predators to reproduce in greater numbers, so birds with a life cycle that is a factor of the cicadas' would be in abundance the next time they emerged. This could establish a rhythm, resulting in lots of predators regularly being around in years when there were lots of prey. But a prime-numbered life cycle avoids that problem.

Female cicadas must pick a healthy tree in which to lay their eggs (to the vexation of orchard owners, whose trees can be weakened by the cicadas). They deposit them in the tree's branches. When they hatch two weeks later, the larvae fall to the ground. They then tunnel down to the tree's roots, from which they suck out their sustenance. If a female chooses poorly and the tree dies in the next 17 years, her larvae will perish too. They will also do badly if the tree has old, gnarled roots, rather than young, succulent ones. This may explain why cicadas do well in suburban areas, where trees tend to be young, healthy and face less competition for resources than they might in a thicket.

Learning about the members of Brood X is a painstaking process, not least because they emerge only every 17 years. Entomologists have been gathering data on this group for more than a century, but modern technology gave them a helping hand this time around. Mr Kritsky had developed an app called Cicada Safari through which the public could upload cicada sightings, helping to map the creatures' emergence and habitats. In 2021 the sound of smartphone cameras snapping was audible alongside the cicadas' calls. Who knows what the world will look like when they next emerge, in 2038?

What do genes reveal about the settlement of Pacific islands?

The colonisation of the Pacific Ocean was one of the great feats of human navigation. Groups of a few dozen people, travelling in canoes carved from trees, discovered and settled hundreds of tiny islands separated by vast spans of open water. They found their way using the stars, dead reckoning and study of the wind and waves. Exactly when these trips occurred, and in which order, is unclear. Oral histories are richly detailed, but vague on dates. The colonisers moved too fast for linguistic analysis to yield answers. Archaeological evidence is scant. But a paper by Alex Ioannidis of Stanford University and 26 other scholars claims to have clarified this fuzzy history using genetics, by analysing the DNA of 430 modern-day Polynesians.

Polynesian prehistory reaches back to the island now called Taiwan. From there, starting in around 2500BC, the ancestors of today's Pacific Islanders are thought to have spread through the Philippines and Indonesia to western Polynesian islands such as Samoa and Fiji. They paused there for centuries or more, before venturing on to the vast emptiness of the Pacific. The authors focus on this second expansion.

The team relied on a genetic pattern called the "founder effect". Each canoe probably carried only a few dozen people, out of hundreds or thousands living on the originating island. These pioneers' descendants should thus be less genetically diverse than people on the island from which their ancestors came. Every subsequent colonisation should have created a new genetic bottleneck. The authors determined the order of the voyages by finding this signature in modern genomes, while excluding confounding chunks of DNA contributed by later arrivals from Europe.

The dates are less certain than the sequence. Genomics counts time in generations, not years. However, research on other places in pre-modern time periods, such as 17th-century Iceland and rural

The settlement of Polynesia
Reconstructed from the genes
of modern inhabitants

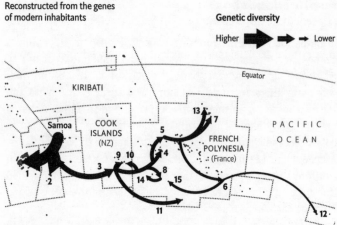

1 Fiji, too early to date **2** Tonga, too early to date **3** Rarotonga, 830AD **4** Tahiti, 1050 **5** Pallisers, 1110
6 Mangareva, 1130 **7** South Marquesas, 1140 **8** Tubuai, 1150 **9** Atiu, 1190 **10** Mauke, 1190 **11** Rapa Iti,
1190 **12** Easter Island, 1210 **13** North Marquesas, 1330 **14** Rimatara, 1340 **15** Raivavae, 1360

How gene variants were lost during colonisation

The founder effect

A small group travels to a new island.
By chance none of them has a variant
found in the original population, so
their descendants lack this variant.

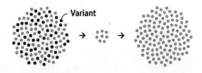

Genetic drift

A variant becomes less common over
generations due to random chance, and is
eventually lost from the gene pool. This is
more likely to occur in a small population.

Source: "Paths and timings of the peopling of Polynesia inferred
from genomic networks", by A. Ioannidis et al., *Nature*, 2021

Quebec in the 1800s, suggests an average generation length of 30 years. The study shows that the Polynesians moved quickly once they set out into open ocean. One of the first colonisation voyages probably set off in around 830AD from Samoa to Rarotonga – the largest of the Cook Islands, a speck of 67 square kilometres about 1,500km to the south-east. By 1050, explorers seem to have reached Tahiti. Just 50 years later, they had probably set foot in the Tuamotu Islands, a series of tiny atolls 1,500km long. A heroic 2,600km journey from Mangareva to Easter Island, one of the remotest dots of land on the planet, is likely to have occurred in around 1210.

This chronology is of course inexact. However, the authors are confident in the sequence, and say that the total dating error should be only around 60 years. Moreover, their account is compatible with both archaeological records and Polynesians' own oral histories. In more ways than one, the history of the Polynesian voyagers lives on in their descendants.

Why are there so many missions to Mars?

Mars is awash with alien technology. Alien to Mars, that is. On February 18th 2021 NASA's *Perseverance* rover landed in a crater called Jezero, near the planet's equator, after travelling 470m kilometres over seven months. The United Arab Emirates' *Hope* orbiter had gone into orbit around the planet a few days earlier. China's *Tianwen-1* entered Mars orbit a day later, and its lander and rover touched down in May. There were already six operational satellites in orbit around Mars when *Hope* arrived, and *Perseverance* joined two operational probes on the surface, NASA's *Curiosity* rover and *InSight* lander, which arrived in 2012 and 2018, respectively. Why are there so many Mars missions – and what do countries that send them hope to achieve?

In the 1890s Percival Lowell, an American astronomer, fixed a telescope on Mars and observed a network of long straight lines that he believed to be canals built by an alien civilisation. In the second half of the 20th century, orbiters circling the planet returned far more detailed data about its atmosphere and surface, putting an end to the theory that a race of Martians had existed. But subsequent missions instead raised new questions about alien life. They showed that once Mars was more like Earth. Streams, river valleys, basins and deltas on the planet's surface suggest there may have been water covering its northern hemisphere. Orbiters, landers and rovers have set out to explore the planet's topography and probe its interior for decades in the hopes of revealing whether microbial life might have existed in the past – and whether it still exists today.

There were roughly 50 years of Mars missions before *Perseverance*. NASA, America's space agency, was the first to land a craft successfully on its surface, in 1976. The latest flurry of activity is down to two things: new opportunities to answer questions about life beyond Earth, and astropolitical grandstanding. *Perseverance* is studying the planet's geological record and looking for chemical traces of ancient microbial life, whereas the UAE's *Hope* orbiter will help scientists to understand how gas escapes its atmosphere – a process that has made Mars cold and dry. Technological advances mean that samples collected by *Perseverance* could eventually be brought back to Earth, allowing more detailed analysis.

But space exploration is also a matter of prestige and techno-nationalism. China's growing space race with its neighbours, India and Japan, which have also sent probes to Mars, reflects their jostling for influence on Earth. The UAE, whose space agency was founded only in 2014, has crowed that its *Hope* orbiter is the first interplanetary mission by any Arab country. This posturing is a far cry from the white-hot space rivalry between America and the Soviet Union during the cold war, and there is plenty of collaboration too: NASA is working with the European Space Agency to retrieve samples collected by *Perseverance*, for example. But the number of new spacefaring countries reflects a diffusion of wealth, technology and power.

As well as the UAE, lots of other countries have founded space agencies since 2010, including Australia, Mexico, New Zealand, Poland, Portugal, South Africa and Turkey. For now, states have a monopoly on Mars. But billionaires want in too. Elon Musk, the boss of SpaceX, a private rocketry firm, claims he will launch people to Mars by 2026. Jeff Bezos stepped down as the chief executive of Amazon partly to focus on his space venture, Blue Origin (though he prefers the idea of floating space colonies to dusty rocks like Mars). One day a trip to Mars may be more about leisure than scientific endeavour. As *Perseverance* scours the planet's surface for clues of ancient life, Earthlings also have plans to move in.

What counts as a journey into space?

On July 20th 2021 Jeff Bezos, the owner of Blue Origin, a rocket maker, was one of the first people to ride into space in the RSS *First Step*, the company's reusable space capsule. Nine days earlier Sir Richard Branson, a British billionaire and the founder of Virgin Galactic, had been one of the passengers on VSS *Unity*, a spaceplane that made a suborbital flight. Neither vehicle went into orbit – indeed, neither even left the Earth's atmosphere. So why were these flights counted as journeys into space?

The answer is the altitude. The thinner the atmosphere, the faster a winged aircraft must move if it is to stay aloft. In the 1950s a pioneering aeronautical engineer, Theodore von Kármán, pointed out that there must be an altitude at which the air is so thin that the speed needed for aerodynamic flight is higher than the speed needed to go into orbit – that is, for the combination of its forward momentum and the Earth's gravitational attraction to keep the vehicle going round the planet. Calculations suggested that this disjuncture – now known as the von Kármán line – sat about 100km above the Earth.

Various bodies, including the Fédération Internationale Aéronautique, subsequently decreed that to pass that 100km line was to enter space. The RSS *First Step* was moving fast enough by the time its engines cut out about 40km above the Earth to coast all the way up to that boundary before falling back down. As well as taking the passengers up over the von Kármán line, this parabolic trajectory also provided them with some of the signature experiences of space flight – a black sky, a clearly curved horizon, and a few minutes of the weightlessness that comes with free fall. Mr Bezos thinks that selling this experience to rich thrill- and status-seekers will be a nice business.

But the 100km definition is not universally accepted. America's air force treats 50 miles (roughly 80km) as the edge of space, a definition that allowed it to give astronaut wings to five pilots of its X-15 experimental rocket plane in the 1960s. Jonathan McDowell, an astrophysicist at Harvard who takes a keen interest in spaceflight, has calculated that, in practice, the von Kármán line is closer to 80km than 100km, and that this might be the more defensible definition. That suits Virgin Galactic, which has spent over a decade developing rocket-powered aeroplanes that will offer similar suborbital thrills. VSS *Unity* reached an altitude of 89km on a test flight in May 2021, and 86km on its flight in July, with Sir Richard aboard. Its passengers also enjoyed views of a black sky and a curved horizon, and a few minutes of weightlessness.

A third billionaire went into space for rather longer, later in the year. Jared Isaacman, who made his money as boss of Shift4, a payments company, contracted with SpaceX, a company which ferries astronauts to and from the International Space Station, for a three-day orbital trip in one of its Dragon capsules with three other passengers. Going into orbit is a question of speed as well as altitude: to remain in orbit a vehicle must reach an altitude of at least 200km with a transverse velocity (ie, relative to the Earth's surface) of at least 25,000kph. That is far beyond the capabilities of the Blue Origin and Virgin Galactic vehicles. But by some definitions at least, the joyrides they provide count as journeys into space.

What is a supermoon?

Some rudimentary knowledge of astronomy is required to point out the constellations, and identify the bright planets Venus, Mars, Jupiter and Saturn. But the Moon is unmissable and unmistakable. In recent years, however, a distinction has increasingly been made between an ordinary Moon and a supposedly more special variety: a "supermoon", when the Moon may seem larger and brighter than usual because of its proximity to Earth. What exactly is a supermoon, and how noticeable is it?

The term "supermoon" was first used in 1979 by American astrologer Richard Nolle, to describe a Moon that is full – when it is directly opposite the Sun, as seen from Earth, and its near side is thus fully illuminated – at the same time that it reaches the closest point to Earth in its orbit. (The technical name is a perigee-syzygy Moon: perigee referring to its closest point, and syzygy being the term for three or more astronomical bodies arranging themselves in a straight line.) As it moves along its elliptical orbit, the Moon's distance from Earth varies between about 360,000km (223,694 miles) and 400,000km. At perigee the Moon's centre is on average around 363,300km from Earth. Not everyone agrees on exactly how close to full the Moon needs to be at perigee (or how close to perigee the Moon needs to be when full) to count as a supermoon, however. So whether a particular full Moon is a supermoon, and how frequently supermoons occur, both depend on who you ask.

Some astronomers sneer at the term supermoon because the difference between a supermoon and an average full Moon is almost indistinguishable to the naked eye. An apogee-syzygy Moon – the opposite of a supermoon, dubbed a "micromoon" – occurs when the Moon is full at the farthest point from Earth in its orbit. A full Moon at its perigee appears around 7% larger and 15% brighter than an average full Moon, and 14% larger and 30% brighter than one at its apogee. It may be noticeable in other ways, however. Particularly strong "spring tides" occur during either a full or a new Moon, when the Sun, Earth and the Moon line up and the Sun's gravity reinforces the Moon's gravity.

Moreover, when a full moon appears especially large it may be because of the "Moon illusion", a trick of the eye when the Moon is close to the horizon. A possible explanation is that, when seen with buildings, mountains or trees surrounding it, the Moon appears comparatively larger. Or it could simply be that our brains trick us into thinking that things low on the horizon look bigger than things high in the sky. Either way, a supermoon is not quite as super as its name suggests.

Did insufficient infrastructure doom the first electric cars?

"All is rotary, beautifully perfect and wonderfully efficient," said one evangelist for electric vehicles (EVs). "There is not that almost terrifying uncertain throb and whirr of the powerful combustion engine ... no dangerous and evil smelling gasoline and no noise. Perfect freedom from vibration assures both comfort and peace of mind." Such views would not sound out of place from Elon Musk, the chief executive of Tesla. But their author was Thomas Edison, his predecessor as America's most famous inventor, in 1903.

Then as now, EVs posed a competitive threat to petrol-powered cars. In 1905 most commercial vehicles were EVs. Ads aimed at affluent women touted EVs' cleanliness, ease of use and lack of exhaust. (Petrol-powered vehicles, which offered better performance but were more complicated to operate and maintain, were assumed to be for men only.) Yet by the 1920s, EVs were a dying breed. The standard account of their demise is that drivers were put off by their limited range and higher cost, relative to petrol-powered cars. But a paper by Josef Taalbi and Hana Nielsen of Lund University argues that their main disadvantage was instead a lack of infrastructure.

The authors consider various causes of petrol vehicles' triumph between 1900 and 1910. Cost is unlikely, since until 1910 petrol-powered cars and EVs of the same model type were similarly priced. As for range, some EVs managed a respectable 90 miles (145km) by the 1910s. Had this been EVs' principal handicap, battery-swapping stations, which replaced depleted batteries with charged ones in seconds, could have become as common as petrol stations.

To test other explanations, the authors analysed the specifications and production sites of 37,000 model-year pairs of American cars in the period 1895–1942. Although petrol-powered cars were the most common, their market share varied by location. In places with the infrastructure EVs needed – smooth roads, which reduced jostling of heavy batteries, and ample electricity

Unplugged
American cars manufactured between 1900 and 1942

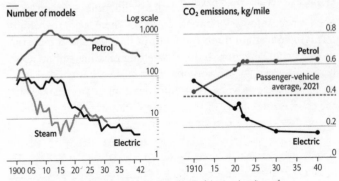

Sources: "The role of energy infrastructure in shaping early adoption of electric and gasoline cars",
by J. Taalbi and H. Nielsen, *Nature Energy*, 2021

– production of EVs was more common. In areas without such capacity, petrol predominated. The infrastructure needs of petrol vehicles were largely met before they were invented, because many rural stores already stocked gasoline as a cleaning fluid, or as a fuel for farm equipment.

The study then used a statistical model to predict how automotive history might have differed if the power grid had developed faster. It finds that if the amount of electricity America produced by 1922 had been available in 1902, 71% of car models in 1920 would have been EVs (though long-distance motorists would still have chosen petrol cars). Accounting for the extra power generation such a fleet would need, this would have cut America's carbon-dioxide emissions from cars in 1920 by 44%.

A century later, the quantity and speed of charging stations still limit purchases of EVs by drivers worried about long trips. The infrastructure gap, however, is narrowing. Tesla, the leading maker of electric cars, has set up 25,000 speedy "superchargers" (though only Tesla drivers can use them). And a bipartisan bill passed by

America's Senate in 2021 includes $7.5bn to boost charging capacity. The study suggests that today, like a century ago, more support for EV infrastructure could have an outsized impact.

What is the metaverse?

Facebook plans to hire 10,000 people in the EU over the next five years to build a metaverse. The company announced its plans in October 2021 – and its boss, Mark Zuckerberg, also said his firm would be changing its name to Meta to signal that it is now a "metaverse company". Plenty of other tech bigwigs have similar ambitions. Tim Sweeney, the boss of Epic Games, the company behind "Fortnite", a popular video game, has said he aims "to build something like a metaverse from science fiction". And Jensen Huang, the boss of Nvidia, an American chipmaker, told *Time* magazine that he wants to create "a virtual world that is a digital twin of ours". What is a metaverse, and how might one be built?

The word comes from *Snow Crash*, published in 1992, the third novel by Neal Stephenson, an American science-fiction author. The book's main character, Hiro Protagonist, delivers pizza for the Mafia, which now controls territory in what used to be the United States. When not working, Mr Protagonist plugs into the Metaverse: a networked virtual reality in which people appear as self-designed "avatars" and engage in activities both mundane (conversation, flirting) and extraordinary (sword fights, mercenary espionage). Like the internet, Mr Stephenson's Metaverse is a collective, interactive endeavour that is always on and is beyond the control of any one person. As in a video game, people inhabit and control characters that move through space.

As is often the case, this sci-fi vision has inspired techies to try to build it for real. (Never mind that Mr Stephenson's novel is dystopian and warns of the dangers of such a parallel virtual world.) Think of it as a reboot of virtual reality, or a massively multiplayer online game (MMOG or more commonly MMO) combined with entertainment and social media. The idea is that people could play games, but they could also talk, shop, stroll, chat, watch movies, attend concerts, shop and do most things that they can do in the real world – and, crucially, the metaverse would connect with the real world in countless unpredictable ways. This fully formed metaverse remains a long way off. But some MMOs have already shown multiversal tendencies. Musicians including Travis Scott and Ariana Grande have staged multimedia performances inside "Fortnite" that were attended by millions of people, for example.

To Silicon Valley dreamers, this immersive, networked, three-dimensional world will eventually succeed the two-dimensional internet that exists today. People who have grown up with "Minecraft" and "Roblox" may already regard the internet as an online world, rather than a set of pages or apps. But a three-dimensional internet will require infrastructure, technical standards and processing power that do not yet exist, able to sustain countless live, synchronous connections. Just as connecting computers and networks in the 1990s made new things possible, however, perhaps connecting up today's various virtual worlds would also open new doors. It may sound like pie in the virtual sky. But with the pandemic having prompted millions of people to spend their days living and working in online video calls, a more sophisticated and realistic alternative may have appeal. The metaverse is certainly closer to reality than it was when Mr Stephenson first dreamed it up.

Why is the "right to repair" gadgets and machines spreading?

It was quite the volte-face. On November 17th 2021 Apple announced that it would give customers "who are comfortable with completing their own repairs" access to specialised tools and parts to fix their broken iPhones. Right up until its announcement, the firm had been vigorously defending its long-standing policy of allowing only its technicians or licensed workshops to tinker with its products. In the past it has even disabled iPhones that had been repaired by other means. To start with, Apple's new policy applies only to certain repairs, such as cracked screens and flat batteries in its latest models – and only for customers in America. But the firm says it will roll out the scheme to more products and countries.

Apple's change of heart is being seen as a victory for a growing "right to repair" movement. Around the world, organisations such as The Repair Association, an American advocacy group, have been fighting manufacturers' tendencies to bar people from fixing their own goods, whether smart gadgets, cars or washing machines. Carmakers are coming under increasing pressure. John Deere, a tractor manufacturer, is embroiled in a long-running row with farmers, many of whom have downloaded unofficial software for their vehicles so that they can make repairs without going through a costly authorised dealership.

Right to repair is a popular cause. A YouGov survey carried out in October 2021, for example, found that 81% of Britons would support the expansion of right-to-repair legislation to include smartphones, tablets and laptops (it already covers things such as white goods and televisions). Politicians seem to be on board too. In America, 27 states are considering right-to-repair legislation, according to the US Public Interest Research Group (US PIRG), a lobby group, although none has yet passed into law. The European Parliament has voted to beef up regulation in the EU, so that certain new electrical goods will need to be repairable for at least ten years.

The pandemic seems to have added urgency to the cause.

Under lockdown, not only did people splurge more on gadgets, but many found their local dealers closed when those devices needed fixing. On occasion proprietary servicing became a matter of life and death. According to US PIRG, hospital technicians became exasperated when they found they could not quickly fix ventilators in overflowing intensive-care units because they did not have immediate access to manuals and parts. This prompted several manufacturers, such as GE, to make more service materials freely available.

The arguments for allowing greater right to repair are compelling. The first is a sense of moral justice. As The Repair Association's slogan puts it, "We have the right to repair everything we own." The second is to stop price-gouging. One reason firms are so keen to maintain a monopoly on fixing the items they produce is that they can charge inflated prices for parts and labour. That in turn encourages so-called "planned obsolescence". When the cost of changing a worn-out smartphone battery is a high fraction of the price of buying a new device, consumers are inevitably nudged towards the latter. In the YouGov survey, a quarter of respondents said they had thrown away their last gadget without trying to repair it. That is good for firms, but bad for the environment. Apple says that 80% of its emissions come from the manufacturing process.

It is this last appeal to greater sustainability – alongside the threat of legislation – that appears to be convincing firms to play ball. Despite all this, consumers may still find self-repair difficult. From Teslas to tractors, doorbells to dishwashers, goods are becoming more complicated, stuffed more with impenetrable computer chips than cogs. Admittedly, there are "how to" guides for almost everything on YouTube these days. Even so, anyone lacking an insider's knowledge of what makes modern gadgets tick may still find themselves locked out.

How has the pandemic affected the gender gap in academic research?

When the covid-19 pandemic first shut down campuses in America and Europe in 2020, the reactions among academics were mixed. Some were thrilled to retreat to home offices with uninterrupted time for thinking, writing and analysis. Many others bemoaned the disruptions to work caused by home-schooling and child-care responsibilities. "The next person who tweets about how productive Isaac Newton was while working from home gets my three-year-old posted to them," joked one researcher. Studies have shown that, across many professions, the disturbances caused by enforced home-working did not affect all workers equally. Even before the pandemic, women shouldered most of the domestic chores. The pandemic only reinforced this trend. Between February and April 2020, women in America scaled back the hours they spent on professional duties up to five times more than men did. No surprise, then, that the first wave of the pandemic coincided with a drop in the proportion of papers submitted by female academics.

A study by a group of European researchers examined papers by over 5m authors submitted to journals owned by Elsevier, an academic publisher that accounts for about 16% of the market – more than any other company. Between February and May 2020 the number of papers submitted surged by 30% compared with the same period in 2019. But the increase in submissions from men outstripped that from women. On average about 20 additional papers were submitted for every 100 female researchers, but more than 25 for men. This widened an already large gender gap, where submissions from women accounted for less than one-third of the total in 2019.

The pattern was the same across all the research fields examined, from engineering to economics. But the effect was particularly pronounced for academics who were at an earlier stage in their careers, and most likely to have young children or to be caring for frail parents. Those responsibilities surged during the pandemic,

The covid-19 ceiling

Academic papers published in journals owned by Elsevier, a publisher

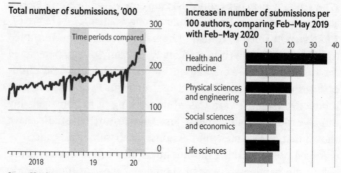

Total number of submissions, '000

Time periods compared

Increase in number of submissions per 100 authors, comparing Feb–May 2019 with Feb–May 2020

Health and medicine

Physical sciences and engineering

Social sciences and economics

Life sciences

Source: "Gender gap in journal submissions and peer review during the first wave of the covid-19 pandemic. A study on 2329 Elsevier journals", by F. Squazzoni et al., *PLoS ONE*, 2021

when schools were closed and elderly people were encouraged to stay indoors. One area in which women's contributions to academia remained steady was in peer-reviews. That suggests that they prioritised work for journals over their own research. But academics are often judged on the quantity of papers they produce. In a world where researchers must "publish or perish", and where women are already under-represented at the top table, the smaller share of publications could have a damaging effect on women's career progression.

Game theory: unexpected results in sport

How do footballers get their shirt numbers?

In 2009, Cristiano Ronaldo moved from Manchester United to Real Madrid in a deal worth £80m ($130m at the time), then a record transfer fee for a footballer. In 2021 he returned to the English club, at the age of 36, for a knockdown £12.85m ($17.6m). But it was uncertain whether Ronaldo (whose full name is Cristiano Ronaldo dos Santos Aveiro) could keep his famous number, seven. The number was first given to him by Sir Alex Ferguson, Manchester United's manager, when Ronaldo joined the club in 2003, and since then he has worn it every season bar one, when he moved to Madrid. Premier League rules state that a player must retain his number throughout the season, however, and Edinson Cavani had already started in the seven shirt for United that season. But the league agreed to make an exception for Ronaldo. How do footballers get their shirt numbers?

When club football became popular in England in the 19th century, players would appear without a number. Instead they were identified by their position on the pitch. Teams almost always played in a 2-3-5 formation (two fullbacks, three halfbacks and five forwards, plus a goalkeeper), and substitutes were not permitted, so tracking players was easy. The first record of shirt numbers at club level was in August 1928, when Arsenal and Chelsea wore them in matches against Sheffield Wednesday and Swansea Town, respectively. England's national team didn't don numbers officially until 1937, when they beat Norway 6–0 in Oslo. In 1939 the Football League Management Committee, the sport's governing body in England, voted that all clubs must number their players' shirts from one to 11. From 1965 a substitute was allowed to wear 12, and when a second substitute was permitted from 1987 they usually played in 14 (13 being thought unlucky).

Numbers one to 11 corresponded to how the 2-3-5 formation would appear in newspaper reports and matchday programmes. It scanned down the page: the goalkeeper wore number one, right back two, left back three, etc, down to the attacking left winger

---

Got your number

at 11. These numbers largely endured as tactics changed from a 2-3-5 formation to 4-4-2, which arranged the team in lines of four defenders, four midfielders and two strikers. This meant there was no longer a strict link between positions and shirt numbers. And not every country's tactics evolved identically. For example, Hungary's national side in the 1950s numbered its defenders from two to four, with five playing in midfield, rather than in defence as was common in England. In 1953 England lost to Hungary by six goals to three in part because the English players struggled with opposite numbers in unexpected positions. Argentina's 1978 World Cup squad, meanwhile, was numbered alphabetically (apparently to avoid arguments), so Norberto Alonso, a midfielder, wore the number one usually reserved for goalkeepers.

In 1993 the Premier League scrapped the old system and required each member of a squad to keep his number for an entire season regardless of position, largely to make it easier to identify players. In that season 37 different numbers appeared. Other leagues quickly followed suit. (In international tournaments, such as the World Cup, each player in a squad is assigned a number for the tournament.) Managers tend to dish out the sought-after low numbers to the best players, a legacy of the "first 11" line-up, indicating that they will start regularly. Number nine, usually worn by the centre forward, is often coveted by goalscorers. And some players, such as Ronaldo, make a number their own off the pitch as well as on it. Products adorned with his CR7 branding include underwear, shoes, deodorant and a string of hotels.

How did empty stadiums affect footballers' performance?

"To the 'people' ... who made the monkey noises: Shame on you. Shame on you", posted Mario Balotelli, then a striker for Brescia, on Instagram in late 2019. He was referring to fans of Hellas Verona, a rival football club, who hurled racist abuse at him that exceeded even the typical taunts from overheated "ultras". At one point during the match, play was suspended as a distraught Mr Balotelli punted the ball at jeering hecklers and threatened to walk off the pitch. Mr Balotelli did manage to score a goal that day, though Brescia still lost 2–1. However, recent research by Fabrizio Colella, an economics graduate student at the University of Lausanne, suggests that the striker's strong performance in the face of racist abuse was more an exception than a rule.

By forcing sports teams to play games without fans, the covid-19 pandemic created a compelling natural experiment that has unleashed a flurry of academic research. Many studies, including one published last year in *The Economist*, have sought to measure how much of home teams' advantage comes from the presence of supporters. Mr Colella, however, made use of the new data to examine a question with broader social implications. All footballers get heckled, but not all of them suffer the same types of insults. At least in European stadiums, fans single out non-white players for racially tinged attacks. Do such barbs sting more than the standard battery of non-racial abuse suffered by white players?

The pandemic allowed Mr Colella to find out. For each player in Serie A, the top tier of Italian football, he compiled individual performance scores in every match during the previous two years ranging from zero to ten. (These numbers take into account contributions in all aspects of the game, not just offensive statistics like goals or assists.) Next, he classified over 500 players as either white or non-white using the Fitzpatrick scale for human skin colour, which is commonly used in dermatology research. Finally, he compared how each player fared, on average, in matches played

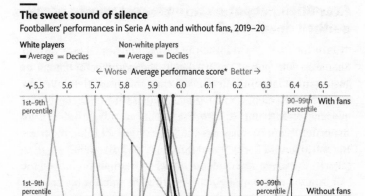

The sweet sound of silence
Footballers' performances in Serie A with and without fans, 2019–20

White players
■ Average ▬ Deciles

Non-white players
■ Average ▬ Deciles

← Worse Average performance score* Better →

⌁5.5 5.6 5.7 5.8 5.9 6.0 6.1 6.2 6.3 6.4 6.5

1st–9th percentile   90–99th percentile **With fans**

1st–9th percentile   90–99th percentile **Without fans**

30–39th percentile for **non-white players**, eg Mario Balotelli

On average, **non-white players** performed better without a crowd

90–99th percentile for **white players**, eg Cristiano Ronaldo

Sources: Fabrizio Colella; fantacalcio.it   *Fantacalcio algorithmic match-level fantasy-football score

in front of fans against their performances in empty stadiums. Although fans may affect results in many ways, only racist chants could plausibly have a different impact on white players than on non-white ones.

The results were striking. On average, white players scored slightly worse without fans than they did in packed stadiums. In contrast, non-white footballers' performances improved to a statistically significant degree when fans were absent, by an average of 1.2%. Mr Colella built a mathematical model that tried to account for these differences using other variables, such as players' nationalities and teams' overall quality. However, none of these controls eliminated the impact of skin colour. The effect was greater for the darkest-skinned players. Perhaps the only thing more dispiriting than the scourge of racist abuse in top-flight international football is the notion that it might actually work.

Are penalty shoot-outs the fairest way to break football deadlocks?

In 1976 the final of the European Championships was settled by football's most famous penalty. After 120 minutes of playing time had failed to separate Czechoslovakia and West Germany, the match went to a penalty shoot-out, the first time it had been tried in a major tournament. With the Czechs already ahead 4–3, up stepped Antonín Panenka. Feinting to put the ball into the corner, and waiting until the German goalkeeper had dived full-length to his left, the Czech midfielder delicately – daringly – chipped the ball into the centre of the goal, securing the title for his country. To this day spot kicks taken (and often missed) in this fashion are known as "Panenkas". Penalty shoot-outs such as the one in 1976 are memorable, nerve-jangling spectacles. But are they a fair way of deciding a football match?

The format is simple. If, in a knockout tournament, two teams remain tied after the regulation 90 minutes and then 30 minutes' extra time, the match goes to penalties. Each side chooses five players to take alternating spot kicks, with the team that scores the most winning. If they are still tied, the remaining players take turns in a sudden-death competition. The pressure can get to even the most revered footballers. In the World Cup final in 1994, for example, Roberto Baggio, Italy's superstar forward (and a famously meditative Buddhist), blazed his side's fifth penalty over the bar, handing the title to Brazil. Indeed shoot-outs are such levellers that they are often described as lotteries. Studies have found little evidence that they favour better sides.

There are two ways to come up with a fairer tiebreaker. The first is to improve the shoot-out format itself. When teams take alternate attempts at goal (ie, ABAB), the team going first has been proven to have a significant advantage. It wins around 60% of the time, according to a study from the London School of Economics (though other studies have found slightly smaller effects, which betting markets tend to reflect). That is probably down to the psychological pressure on the players shooting second, who must often score to keep their side's hopes alive. (The decision on who goes first is made by coin toss.) FIFA, football's governing body, has trialled an ABBA sequence. This is the same format used in tennis tiebreakers. But the experiment was not deemed a success, in part because supporters found it confusing. Heaven knows, then, how they would cope with the Prouhet–Thue–Morse mathematical constant. This sequence, ABBABAAB, is considered the fairest for penalty shoot-outs – and many other duels besides, including playing white in a chess tournament. Experiments suggest that using Prouhet–Thue–Morse levels up a team's chances in a shoot-out to about 50–50. (Drummers will recognise the pattern as an inverted paradiddle.)

But an equal chance merely evens up the lottery. The second way to give the more deserving side the better chance of winning is to do away with penalties altogether. But how? One option is a different kind of shoot-out, in which players dribble the ball from the centre circle and have a set amount of time to beat the goalkeeper (sometimes an outfield defender is also added). This may require more skill than merely shooting from 12 yards. The "golden goal", in which teams win if they score first in extra time, was tried and ditched because it encouraged defensive football from sides petrified of offering chances to the opposition. Perhaps the most compelling idea is a form of golden goal in which there is no limit on extra time, but a player from each side is removed at regular intervals (every ten minutes, say). The resulting extra space – and fatigue – would, the idea goes, lead to more chances to score.

And yet for many fans, it is exactly the idea that an underdog might cling on doggedly during a match and then beat a mightier opponent in a randomised tiebreaker that constitutes the whole appeal of the shoot-out. Those unfancied Czechs who halted the West German juggernaut in 1976 set a precedent in this regard too.

Which countries cheat the most in athletics?

Alongside the visible sporting contest of the 2020 Olympics in Tokyo, held in 2021, sat a hidden, pharmacological one. Away from the TV cameras, in laboratories and huts and cubicles, anti-doping officials were scouring samples from the 11,482 athletes at the games, looking for evidence of any one of the hundreds of banned performance-enhancing drugs. Even before the games, athletes were visited by officials conducting surprise out-of-competition tests. No one knows how many athletes use chemical enhancement, although most experts agree it is widespread. Estimates vary from sport to sport, and range from 10% to 40%. But track-and-field athletics – one of the centrepiece events of the Olympics – has a particularly chequered past.

Of the 12 finalists in the women's 1,500 metres at the 2012 Olympics in London, four were subsequently suspended for doping. In 2013 the entire board of Jamaica's anti-doping agency resigned after it was revealed it had conducted only a single out-of-competition test ahead of the London games. In 2020 Lamine Diack, a former head of the sport's governing body, was sent to prison for corruption and covering up drug-test results. Just before the Tokyo games Shelby Houlihan, an American runner and medal prospect, was barred from the contest after failing a drugs test.

In 2017 the sport set up the Athletics Integrity Unit (AIU), which is independent of the rest of the sport's administration, to police anti-doping. It publishes lists of athletes who have been suspended for doping. If there were an Olympics for doping, Russia would sweep the athletics medal table. Indeed, after a huge state-sponsored doping programme was uncovered in 2016, it was banned, at least in theory, from the Tokyo Games (Russian athletes instead competed as the "Russian Olympic Committee"). Athletes from other ex-Soviet states such as Ukraine, Kazakhstan and Belarus also fall foul of anti-doping officials with striking frequency.

But other entries are perhaps more surprising. East African athletes, especially from Kenya and Ethiopia, have long excelled at

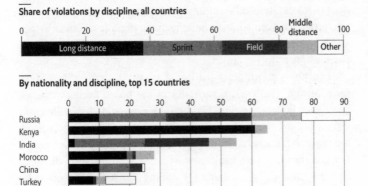

Perhaps it's something in the water

Athletes currently banned from athletics for doping violations, at August 1st 2021

Share of violations by discipline, all countries

Sources: Athletics Integrity Unit; *The Economist*

long-distance running. Their dominance has led sports scientists to publish papers exploring whether people from that part of the world might have some genetic advantage that makes them particularly suitable for endurance events. But recent years have seen a string of doping busts, propelling Kenya and Ethiopia up the pharmacological medal table as well as the Olympic one. At least some of the east African athletes, it seems, have been relying on chemistry as much as genetics.

Different drugs have different effects. Anabolic steroids – close chemical cousins of testosterone, the chief male sex hormone – are best known for building muscle, making them useful in power-focused events like sprints, throwing and jumping. They are particularly effective in women's sports. The women's 100- and 200-metres world records, for instance, were set by Florence Griffith Joyner in 1988, when steroid abuse was rampant and mostly uncontrolled. Even with the benefits of an extra-fast running track and improved shoe technology, no athlete at Tokyo stood much chance of beating her times.

Another perennial favourite is erythropoietin (EPO). Like testosterone, EPO occurs naturally in the body. Taking artificial analogues boosts red-blood cell production, allowing athletes to ferry more oxygen to their muscles. EPO rose to fame in cycling in the 1990s, but is useful in any endurance sport. Many of the banned Kenyan runners were caught using it. As a group, long-distance runners have the most bans for doping violations, followed by sprint-distance athletes (those who compete in races 400 metres or less). Athletes competing in mixed races, such as the pentathlon, and those working in support roles, such as coaching, account for the minority of bans.

Because the AIU's figures reflect only athletes who have been caught, they give only a partial picture of how widespread doping really is. As detection technology improves, athletes will have to adopt new drugs or new strategies to evade the testers. Some of the countries topping the drugs list may be there not because doping is particularly rampant, but because they are less sophisticated than their rivals when it comes to dodging the tests.

Why do so few cities want to host the Olympics?

When Denver pulled out of hosting the 1976 Winter Olympics two years after it was awarded the games, citing financial and environmental worries, it was a shock. Back then, holding the games was seen as a privilege, but now Denver seems ahead of its time. The rush of interested cities has slowed to a trickle, and voters are quickly going off the idea. The International Olympic Committee (IOC) has been forced to revamp its bidding process. Cities are no longer forced to put together proposals costing tens of millions of dollars; the IOC now picks promising candidates and identifies a "preferred bidder". Knockout rounds of voting have been replaced by a more collaborative process. Why do so few cities want to play host? And will the IOC's changes rekindle their interest?

Playing host to the Olympics has come in and out of fashion before. The most common gripe is cost. From the earliest modern games in 1896 until the end of the 1960s, competitions were held in big cities in America and Europe that already had the necessary infrastructure. This kept things cheap. But the games quickly grew. The number of athletes more than doubled between 1956 and 1972. The cost to Montreal, the host of the 1976 summer games, was so exorbitant that the city did not pay off its final debts for the facilities until 2006. Los Angeles was awarded the 1984 games unopposed and negotiated the use of existing infrastructure. The competition was profitable and suddenly the Olympics got its allure back. Emerging markets, such South Korea (1988), Greece (2004) and China (2008), saw it as an opportunity to showcase their development and vitality. But as the number of would-be hosts grew, so did the IOC's list of demands. Hosts needed not only to build world-class sports grounds, but also hotels and metro systems. Revenue from broadcasting rights picked up, but not quickly enough to underwrite the costs. The budget for London's bid for the 2012 games ballooned from a starting point of £2.4bn ($3.3bn) to more than £9.3bn.

Despite the expense, Olympic bids used to be popular with voters. At the end of 2012, eight out of ten Londoners said that the summer's games had been worth the extraordinary cost. But sentiment has shifted. The process for awarding the 2024 games is particularly instructive. In 2015 Boston was the front-runner, until an anti-Olympics campaign helped turn the public against the idea. Of particular concern was a clause in the IOC's contract stipulating that local taxpayers would be responsible if costs overran. When Boston's mayor pulled the plug, Rome, Hamburg and Budapest withdrew their bids too. Eventually only Paris and Los Angeles were left. The IOC took the face-saving step of awarding the games to Paris in 2024 and Los Angeles in 2028. A poll in May found that as many as 80% of Japanese opposed hosting the 2020 games in Tokyo. Many people worried not just about the cost, but the risk to public safety with covid-19 cases rising. Even authoritarian regimes, which care little for voters' objections, may think twice in future about hosting. The games can bring unwanted attention. Hardening attitudes in the West towards human-rights abuses in China fuelled calls to boycott its winter games in 2022 (though in the event the boycott was only diplomatic).

The IOC promised change ahead of the process to award the 2032 games. It said it would make its decision 11 years in advance rather than seven as previously; would consider proposals from groups of cities or whole regions; and would drop the expensive pre-prepared bids in favour of "continuous dialogue" between prospective hosts and a new committee made up mostly of IOC bigwigs. This produced a credible choice in Brisbane, although some German politicians criticised the IOC for a lack of transparency when their bid to host in the Rhine-Ruhr region failed. In truth, the new process gives more control to the IOC. This is likely to result in fewer costly mistakes, but also more accusations of partiality. It also puts much greater pressure on the integrity of its commission members. The IOC has gone from beggar to chooser.

Why sports stars retire early

The surprise decision in March 2022 by Ash Barty, Australia's three-time grand-slam winner, to retire from tennis at the age of 25 provoked much consternation. One commentator even suggested it was indicative of a different attitude towards the work–life balance among millennials. But Ms Barty is far from the first tennis player to quit the sport in her prime. Bjorn Borg was one of the sport's greats, winning five consecutive Wimbledon titles and six French championships. Born in 1956, he was very much a "baby boomer". But he quit tennis at the age of 26 in 1983, having lost the desire to keep playing (he made a short and unsuccessful comeback in the early 1990s). Martina Hingis, a Swiss player with five grand-slam titles, initially retired from the singles tour in 2003 aged just 22.

Perhaps Ms Barty's retirement came as such a shock because the recent trend has been for tennis players to keep going. The big three in the men's game – Roger Federer, Rafael Nadal and Novak Djokovic – were 40, 35 and 34 respectively at the time of her announcement, while Sir Andy Murray was attempting a comeback at 34. On the women's side, 40-year-old Serena Williams has yet to announce her retirement, although she hasn't played since the 2021 Wimbledon tournament. Clearly the competitive urge in some athletes is so strong that they choose to play even when they have earned millions and won every conceivable honour. As for the big three, their rivalry may be keeping them going. After winning the Australian Open in January 2022, Mr Nadal has 21 grand-slam titles whereas Mr Federer and Mr Djokovic have 20 each. To finish ahead of the other two might be the crowning achievement for any of them.

But it is easy to imagine that, for other mortals, success may be almost as great a spur to retire as failure. A couple of tennis grand slams brings financial security for life, plus the scope to keep busy as a media commentator. Tennis involves endless hours of practice and fitness training, as well as ceaseless travel round the globe. Often, a successful tennis player will have started the sport at a very young age and will have had little time to do anything else. Ms Barty had achieved her dream of winning both Wimbledon and her own country's tournament, the Australian Open; perhaps she had no further goal to drive her forward?

The most frequent reason for retirement in many sports is injury. Sandy Koufax, an outstanding baseball pitcher, retired in 1966 at the relatively young age of 30, having just won his third Cy Young award for best pitcher. He gave up in the face of crippling arthritis which had dogged him for the previous two years. "I don't regret for one minute the 12 years I've spent in baseball," he said, "but I could regret one season too many." More recently, Andrew Luck, the quarterback of the Indianapolis Colts, retired at 29 after a long series of injuries that included a torn shoulder, a lacerated kidney and a nagging ankle problem. Contact sports like American football or rugby result in a vast range of injuries. But a non-contact sport like tennis still makes enormous demands of the body. Sir Andy now has a metal hip; Mr Nadal has suffered a long series of injuries, in particular to his left foot; Mr Federer has had back problems and, in recent years, has needed operations on his knees. The scrambling, stretching and chasing involved in tennis puts a lot of strain on the joints. Indeed, the sport has a particular injury (tennis elbow) named after it. The real surprise is not that some stars retire early – it is that they keep going so long.

How cricket is becoming a global game

The opening game of the Men's Twenty20 (T20) Cricket World Cup on October 17th 2021 was hardly a glamour tie. Oman, competing in just its second appearance at the tournament, beat a debutant Papua New Guinea side by a comfortable ten wickets. Still, the International Cricket Council, the sport's governing body, is keen for more such encounters. From 2024 T20 World Cups will be contested by 20 teams, up from 16 in the 2021 line-up.

The ICC recognises three forms of top-tier, international cricket: T20s, a frenzied format lasting just three hours, One Day Internationals (ODIs), and Tests, which are played over five days. T20's fast pace makes it more attractive to broadcasters and therefore advertisers, and the ICC sees it as the ideal format to globalise the game. The more countries that take part, the more money that comes in, and the stronger the case for cricket's return to the Olympics (it was only played once, in 1900, and Britain took the gold).

For most of its 144-year history, international cricket has been an exclusive sport. Today only 12 teams may contest Test matches and 20 compete in ODIs. But in 2018 the ICC awarded T20 international status to all 92 of its non-Test-playing members. This meant any match between members would be regarded as official and the result registered in the global T20 rankings. Between 2018 and 2019, the number of International T20 matches quadrupled. The truncated form of the matches means they are easier to organise and play, which attracts greater participation.

The bigger challenge for smaller countries is money. Of the $2.5bn that the ICC will earn in broadcasting and sponsorship rights for its international tournaments between 2015 and 2023, non-Test-playing members will receive an estimated $2m each.

Smaller countries are still locked out of the most lucrative forms of the sport. The bulk of cricket's global revenues come from matches played by Australia, England and India. Any country that plays against one of the "big three" enjoys a significant windfall.

Racing to the boundary
International men's cricket, by format

Number of matches

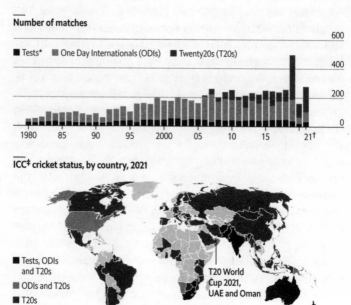

ICC‡ cricket status, by country, 2021

Tests, ODIs
and T20s

ODIs and T20s

T20s

T20 World
Cup 2021,
UAE and Oman

Sources: Cricinfo; ICC   *Played over five days   †To Oct 15th   ‡International Cricket Council

But this triumvirate can generate even bigger profits by playing each other more often. Even traditional cricket-playing countries worry about being excluded from this bonanza. In October 2021 Ramiz Raja, the chairman of Pakistan's cricket board, complained that his country's team depended too heavily on the Indian cricket board. Mr Raja may have felt helpless. But he soon had cause to celebrate – later that month his team beat India by ten wickets in their opening game of the T20 World Cup.

Why are cricket's best captains batsmen?

Few countries have dominated a sport the way Australia has dominated cricket. The national team has won the most Test matches (the traditional five-day format of the game), Ashes series (against its arch-rivals England) and World Cups. In almost all these conquests the Baggy Greens – as the team is known, for the colour of their caps – have been led by a batsman. So when Pat Cummins, a fast bowler, was appointed captain for the Ashes series that began in December 2021, many people were surprised. It was the first time in 65 years a specialist bowler had led the Australian Test team. It was also a rarity in the sport.

Of the 116 skippers since 1880 to have led their teams in more than 15 Tests, only 14 have been bowlers. Another 17 have been "all-rounders", who bat and bowl. Batsmen-captains enjoy longer tenures too. Of the 20 longest-serving skippers, only one was not a specialist batsman: India's Mahendra Singh Dhoni, a wicketkeeper who was also no slouch with the bat. Even in the shorter formats of the game, batsmen dominate in the role.

Captaincy matters in cricket, arguably more than in other sports. Coaches may help in the dressing room but, on the field, captains run the show. They decide the team's strategy, from who bowls when to which fielders stand where. Many in the game feel that batsmen are more naturally suited to these roles. Without the burden of bowling, they have more time to mull over tactics. Some believe that players whose primary role is to bat have a better understanding of field placement. Others worry that bowlers as captains will keep bowling themselves, to the detriment of the team.

At first glance the data support these claims. Of the ten most successful captains, by percentage of games won, nine are batsmen. Steve Waugh, another Australian, tops the list with 72%, ahead of his compatriots Ricky Ponting and Don Bradman. The exception is Waqar Younis, a fierce fast-bowler who led Pakistan with a win rate of 58%. All-rounders have tended to fare worse. Under Garry

Leading from the bat
International men's test cricket captains,* % of matches won

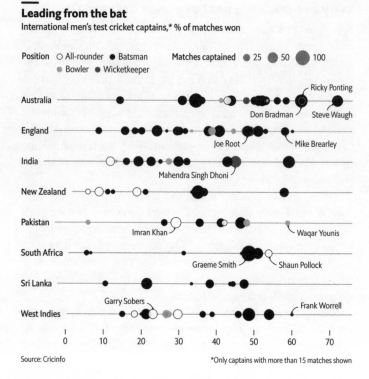

Source: Cricinfo

*Only captains with more than 15 matches shown

Sobers, considered one of the game's greatest, the West Indies won less than a quarter of its Tests.

But a captain's quantity of wins reflects not only his own leadership, but also the quality of his team. Messrs Waugh and Ponting skippered sides packed with brilliant cricketers. No amount of tactical nous can help a captain leading a team of weak players against much stronger opponents. One study that adjusted for team quality found that Mr Waugh was indeed the best captain among those leading games between 1877 and 2010, but Graeme Smith, who led South Africa in the 2000s, was second best, though he won less than half his Tests in the period covered.

And what about the captain's own prowess? Sometimes skill as a leader can compensate for deficiencies as a player. Mike Brearley, who led England in the late 1970s and early 1980s, had a mediocre batting record but still enjoyed a win rate of 60% (and three victorious Ashes series). Some players' form dips under the responsibility of captaincy – for instance, Michael Vaughan, another Ashes-winning England skipper. But some thrive on it. Both the batting and bowling averages of Imran Khan, who went on to become Pakistan's prime minister, were better when he captained the national cricket team than when he didn't, although Pakistan won only 29% of its Tests with him at the helm. Mr Cummins, who started his tenure by dismissing five English batsmen, surely hopes it will be both as personally fruitful as Mr Khan's and as influential as Mr Brearley's.

Cultural questions: arts, media and language

Does South Korea's pop culture make the country more powerful?

The global hype over *Squid Game*, a violent South Korean survival drama released on Netflix in September 2021, revived interest in the relationship between the success of South Korean pop culture and the influence of its government. Much of this analysis presents South Korea's cultural success as an important tool of "soft power" – a state's ability to wield influence in the world by getting other countries to align with its interests without coercion or threat. But does cultural appeal really beget political power?

Governments would like to think so. Moon Jae-in, South Korea's president, is keen to use his country's increasingly hip reputation for political purposes. In April 2018, Mr Moon took a group of K-pop stars to a concert in Pyongyang as part of an effort to improve relations with North Korea. In February 2020 he hosted a celebratory lunch for the director and cast of *Parasite*, which had just won the Oscar for best picture. More recently he appointed the members of BTS, the world's biggest boy band, as "special presidential envoys for future generations and culture". The stars appeared alongside him at the United Nations to promote covid-19 vaccination and sustainable development.

Mr Moon is not the first world leader to hope that co-opting cool kids may have political benefits. During the cold war, both America and the Soviet Union enlisted artists in their ideological confrontation, a practice that prompted Joseph Nye, a political scientist at Harvard, to coin the term "soft power". Tony Blair, Britain's prime minister between 1997 and 2007, invited artists and rock stars to his flat in Downing Street. He sought to capitalise on the appeal of "Cool Britannia", a vague term intended to capture the universal appeal of 1990s British culture in a way not dissimilar to the "Korean wave" branding.

Yet it is hard to tell if such efforts pay off. Some might argue that the global popularity and influence of American pop culture contributed to the demise of the Soviet Union, but the eastern bloc's dysfunctional economic system probably had more to do with it. Soft power is not strong enough to overcome political missteps or weaknesses. The best South Korean film and television draws far too much attention to social problems to lend itself to nationalist PR campaigns. The portrayal of inequality in *Squid Game* was so brutal that a North Korean propaganda outlet used it to illustrate the horrors of life in the South.

The best evidence for the political importance of South Korea's culture may thus be attempts to suppress rather than co-opt it. Since the K-pop gig in Pyongyang, North Korea has tightened its rules against southern tastes and fashions, which it regards as threats to social stability. China has cracked down on video gaming, dealing a blow to what is by far the largest chunk of South Korea's cultural exports. And South Korea itself is no stranger to regarding artists as dangerous renegades. Mr Moon may be courting musicians and film-makers. Previous governments kept blacklists of those whose political views they disliked, cutting them off from state funding. Such policies made life difficult for individual artists, but they did nothing to dampen the popularity of their work. Popular culture proffers political power, but in ways that politicians find difficult to harness.

What does Spotify show about the decline of English?

Bad Bunny may not be a household name in the English-speaking world. Yet the Puerto Rican rapper, whose verses are usually in Spanish (and, on one occasion, Japanese), was the most played artist in 2020 and 2021 for listeners on Spotify, the world's largest music-streaming platform. Such success might have been harder to achieve 30 years ago when English was dominant. In the new digital era, it is becoming ever more common.

To investigate the evolution of music tastes across the world, *The Economist* trawled through the top 100 tracks in 70 countries according to Spotify. Examining 13,000 hits in 70 languages along with other data like genre, lyrical language and nationality of artist, we sought to group countries according to musical similarity. On these 320,000 records, we employed a principal-components analysis to assess the degree of musical kinship between countries, and then a clustering algorithm (known as k-means) to group them. Three broad clusters emerged: a contingent in which English is dominant; a Spanish-language ecosystem; and a third group that mostly enjoys local songs in various tongues. Across all, one trend emerged: the hegemony of English is in decline.

The drop over the past five years is concentrated mostly outside the English sphere. Within the Spanish cluster, English quickly lost ground – from 25% of hits to 14% – as native artists like Bad Bunny and Rauw Alejandro became internationally ascendant. Among the local-language cluster, in countries with strong, indigenous music cultures – like Brazil, France and Japan – English declined even more precipitously, dropping from 52% of hit songs to 30%. Only in the English cluster did the language remain unfazed, falling only slightly from 92% to 90%.

There is no doubt that, despite its decline, English is still king. Of the 50 most-streamed tracks on Spotify over the past five years, 47 were in English. And the genres it incubated are being widely adopted elsewhere. There is now excellent rap available in Arabic,

Tongue-tied

Song language on Spotify, % of total
Among weekly top 100 songs*

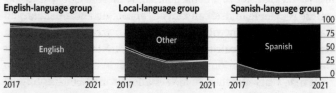

English-language group   Local-language group   Spanish-language group

*To November 12th 2021
Sources: Genius; Google Translate; Musixmatch; Popnable; Soundcharts; Spotify; *The Economist*

Russian and, of course, Spanish. A sign of the momentum in global music tastes comes from a collaboration in 2018 between two superstars – Bad Bunny and Drake, the self-proclaimed king of rap in English. On that occasion, however, Drake delivered the chorus in Spanish.

How did Marvel take over cinema and TV?

Since 1939, Marvel Comics has told hundreds of fantastic tales of superheroes battling to save the planet. But its fight to dominate pop culture is an epic in itself, involving censorship and a bankruptcy that left the company without many of its prized characters. How did Marvel come to rule the movies? And can its superheroes stay on top?

Marvel's first decades were rocky. The comic-book publisher struggled with constant management changes, often over-extending itself and having to cut back. It was also restrained by the Comics Code Authority, a de facto industry regulator that sprung up in America in the 1950s to prevent more intrusive government meddling. Among its many limitations were bans on vampires, "excessive" gunplay and portraying villains sympathetically. In 1986, the company ended up in the hands of Ronald Perelman, a billionaire who took Marvel public three years later. Mr Perelman had big ambitions, calling the company a "mini-Disney".

But after raising too much debt, a poorly judged attempt to invest in the toy business and a downturn in the comic-book market, the company filed for bankruptcy in 1996. Marvel survived the 1990s but was emaciated. It had sold the film and TV rights to its most popular character, Spider-Man, to Sony for less than $10m plus royalties. The rights to other characters, as well as a theme park, were carved up. Over the next decade, Marvel continued to produce comics and helped those who owned the rights to its characters to put them on screen. But the company believed it could do better, and planned to produce and finance its own films.

True to their name, "the Avengers", Marvel's team of superheroes, struck back. The Marvel Cinematic Universe (MCU), a collection of 25 films and four television series released since 2008, has earned over $23bn at the box office, more than twice the amount earned by *Star Wars*, its closest competitor. The series tells a sprawling tale which, like the comics, has no isolated entries or characters. In 2019 *Avengers: Endgame* became the highest grossing film in

Box-office heroes

Marvel Cinematic Universe, box-office revenues, $bn, 2021 prices

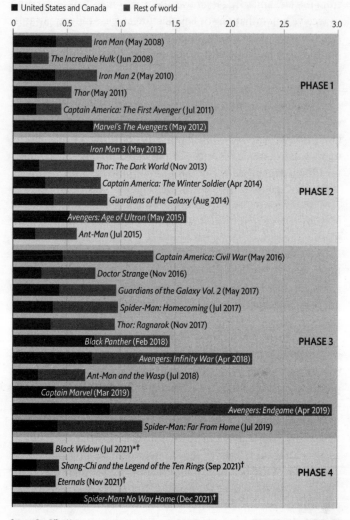

■ United States and Canada   ■ Rest of world

| 0 | 0.5 | 1.0 | 1.5 | 2.0 | 2.5 | 3.0 |

PHASE 1
- Iron Man (May 2008)
- The Incredible Hulk (Jun 2008)
- Iron Man 2 (May 2010)
- Thor (May 2011)
- Captain America: The First Avenger (Jul 2011)
- Marvel's The Avengers (May 2012)

PHASE 2
- Iron Man 3 (May 2013)
- Thor: The Dark World (Nov 2013)
- Captain America: The Winter Soldier (Apr 2014)
- Guardians of the Galaxy (Aug 2014)
- Avengers: Age of Ultron (May 2015)
- Ant-Man (Jul 2015)

PHASE 3
- Captain America: Civil War (May 2016)
- Doctor Strange (Nov 2016)
- Guardians of the Galaxy Vol. 2 (May 2017)
- Spider-Man: Homecoming (Jul 2017)
- Thor: Ragnarok (Nov 2017)
- Black Panther (Feb 2018)
- Avengers: Infinity War (Apr 2018)
- Ant-Man and the Wasp (Jul 2018)
- Captain Marvel (Mar 2019)
- Avengers: Endgame (Apr 2019)
- Spider-Man: Far From Home (Jul 2019)

PHASE 4
- Black Widow (Jul 2021)*†
- Shang-Chi and the Legend of the Ten Rings (Sep 2021)†
- Eternals (Nov 2021)†
- Spider-Man: No Way Home (Dec 2021)†

Sources: Box Office Mojo;
Bureau of Labour Statistics

*Excludes Disney+ PVOD sales
†Released during covid-19 pandemic, not released in China

history (excluding re-releases), taking in $2.8bn. Of the 48 films to have earned more than $1bn at the box office, a fifth have come from the MCU. *Black Panther* was the first comic-book adaptation to receive a nomination for Best Picture at the Academy Awards. And only one of the MCU's films, *Thor,* has received lower than A– on CinemaScore, an audience-rating benchmark. Only Pixar, an animation studio, comes close, with 22 films rated A– or better, but it took more than twice as long to get there.

As the MCU expands, it grows stronger. Over its first five years (Phase 1), the studio released an average of 1.2 films per year and earned $352m (inflation adjusted) per picture in the US and Canada. In 2016–19 (Phase 3), the MCU released 2.75 films per year, earning an average of $483m. In 2021 it released four and broke onto the small screen for the first time, with six TV series. Some growth stems from the support of Walt Disney Company, which acquired Marvel in 2009 for $4bn. Disney's acquisition of 20th Century Fox in 2019 also returned the X-Men and Fantastic Four characters to Marvel, though they have yet to appear in the MCU. In 2016 Sony loaned Spider-Man back to Marvel "because they know what they're doing", according to Tom Rothman, Sony's film boss.

Although other franchises have tried to emulate Marvel's model over the past decade, none has succeeded. But Marvel's growth and cultural influence may have limits. Chinese audiences are increasingly turning to home-grown blockbusters. Marvel may seem unstoppable in the West, but it still faces plenty of battles.

Is the tale of the difficult second novel fact or fiction?

Bettering any success in life can be a daunting task. Not least for successful novelists, who have to tackle the infamous "difficult second novel". Harper Lee, who died in 2016, took five years to publish a second book after her classic of 1960, *To Kill a Mockingbird*. (She actually wrote *Go Set a Watchman* before her famous "first" book, but held onto it for decades.) Viet Thanh Nguyen, an American novelist, says the high expectations and busy schedule following the success of his Pulitzer prize-winning debut, *The Sympathizer*, in 2015 meant that his second book, published earlier this year, was more challenging than the first.

But why do authors supposedly struggle so much with follow-ups? Perhaps it is because novelists feel that they should stay faithful to what readers liked about their first book, while still writing something that is, well, novel. But data from Goodreads, a book-review website, appear to challenge this accepted wisdom. The average rating for a first book from the top 1,000 authors by reviews on the website is 3.87 out of 5. The second book, however, performs slightly better at 3.90 out of 5. Could the notion of the difficult second book be more fiction than reality?

Not necessarily. These headline ratings may well be biased. The group of people who have read and gone on to rate a debut novel may be different to the group who have done so with the second novel. People who enjoyed an author's first book and submitted a review are surely more likely to read and rate a second novel from the same author. Indeed, Goodreads' data show that about one-third of people who gave an author's first book five stars out of five went on to read the second offering. By contrast only 8% of those who gave the book a rating of three stars or fewer read the follow-up. Readers of an author's second book are therefore more likely to enjoy that novelist's writing, which may push up the average rating of an author's second book relative to the first one.

To adjust for these biases *The Economist* has analysed 1.8m

It was a dark and stormy night

Ratings of first and second books by author
Top 250 books by ratings, 0=worst, 5=best

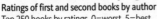
● First book rated higher   ● Second rated higher

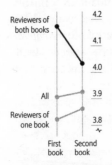

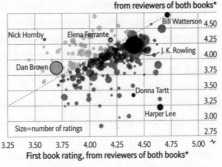

Sources: GoodReads; *The Economist*   *Among people who have rated both books

reviews for 1,116 authors on Goodreads and controlled the scores for whether readers had rated both first and second novels, or just one of the two. We find that the notion of the difficult second novel is, in truth, more fact than fiction. Among reviewers who have read both of an author's books, the average rating (weighted by number of reviews) of the first book is 4.17. The average rating for the second novel falls to 4.03. In many people's eyes, it would still be a decent page-turner.

There are exceptions to the curse of the second novel. Of the 1,100 authors in our dataset, one-third managed to pen a second book that was rated more highly by loyal readers than the first. Nick Hornby, a British author, bettered his 1995 debut novel *High Fidelity*, rated 3.59, with *About a Boy*, released in 1998. The latter has a rating of 4.33 among readers who have read both books. But spare a thought for *Go Set a Watchman*. It suffered the second-highest ratings drop among all the novels in our data, securing a score of just 3.22 – a 30% decline from *To Kill a Mockingbird*.

How has the meaning of the word "woke" evolved?

"Wokeism, multiculturalism, all the-isms – they're not who America is," tweeted Mike Pompeo in 2019 on his last day as America's secretary of state. Until a few years ago "woke" meant being alert to racial injustice and discrimination. Yet in America's fierce culture wars the word is now more likely to be used as a sardonic insult. How did the word turn from a watchword used by black activists to a bogeyman among conservatives?

In 1938 Huddie Ledbetter, a singer, warned black people they "best stay woke, keep their eyes open" going through Scottsboro, Alabama, the scene of a famous mistrial involving nine young black men. The word was first defined in print by William Melvin Kelley, a black novelist, in an article published in the *New York Times* in 1962. Writing about black slang, Mr Kelley defined a "woke" person as someone who was "well-informed, up-to-date". Black people used it in reference to racism and other matters for decades, but the word only entered the mainstream much later. When the Black Lives Matter movement grabbed global attention during anti-racism protests after the killing in 2014 of Michael Brown, an unarmed black teenager, it was inseparable from the phrase "stay woke".

As the word spread into internet culture, thanks in part to the popular #staywoke hashtag, its usage quickly changed. It began to signify a progressive outlook on a host of issues in addition to race. And it was used more often to describe white people active on social media than it was by black activists, who criticised the performatively woke for being more concerned with internet point-scoring than systemic change. Piggybacking corporations, such as Pepsi and Starbucks, lessened the appeal to progressives. Woke's usage went from activist to passé, a common fate of black vernacular terms that make it into the mainstream (other recent victims include "lit" and "on fleek", two terms of praise).

Almost as soon as the word lost its initial sense it found new meaning as an insult – a linguistic process called pejoration.

Becoming a byword for smug liberal enlightenment left it open to mockery. It was redefined to mean "following an intolerant and moralising ideology". The fear of being cancelled by the "woke mob" energised parts of the conservative base. Right-wing parties in other countries noticed that stoking a backlash against wokeness was an effective way to win support.

Another semantic conflict has since emerged over the term "critical race theory", the latest bête noire of the right. What was once an abstruse theory developed in American law schools – one that helped seed core tenets of modern-day wokeism such as intersectionality and systemic racism – has burst into the open. Conservatives panic that it is being taught in schools. Christopher Rufo, a conservative activist, told the *New Yorker* that "'woke' is a good epithet, but it's too broad, too terminal, too easily brushed aside. 'Critical race theory' is the perfect villain." Despite using the same terminology, both sides seem destined to talk past each other. No sooner is one language battle of the culture wars over than another emerges.

How does political correctness relate to press freedom?

Few topics appear to rile people in the West as much as political correctness and its impact on free speech. Although some on the left would like to see more laws governing what is, and is not, acceptable to say in public, most people prefer simply to avoid what they consider hurtful language. Conservatives, meanwhile, tend to complain that this tendency has gone too far and endangers the principle of free speech.

Although people of different political stripes in Western countries rarely find common ground on political correctness, they may have more in common than compatriots in other parts of the world. A survey conducted by Ipsos Mori, a pollster, on behalf of King's College London asked 23,000 adults in 28 countries about their attitudes towards free speech. It asked respondents to rate, on a scale from zero to seven, how they felt about using potentially hurtful words when speaking with people from different backgrounds to their own. A zero would mean that they felt that "people are too easily offended"; a seven would mean they thought it was necessary to "change the way people talk".

More than half of respondents in America, Australia, Britain and Sweden rated themselves between zero and three (excluding those who answered "don't know"), meaning they were the most likely to feel that the general public are too sensitive when it comes to speech. At the other end of the scale, Chinese, Indians and Turks were the least likely to say people were being too sensitive – fewer than one-fifth of the people from these countries responded with a scale of zero to three – instead believing it was necessary to modify their language.

What affects these attitudes across countries? Using an index of press freedom from Reporters Without Borders, a watchdog, *The Economist* found a strong correlation between the extent of press freedom and individual attitudes towards language. Although people living in places with less press freedom are most receptive

The snowflake nations

"Some people think that the way people talk needs to be more sensitive to people from different backgrounds. Others think that many people are just too easily offended. Where would you place yourself on this scale?"

0=people are too easily offended; 7=need to change the way people talk

Overall response, %,* selected countries

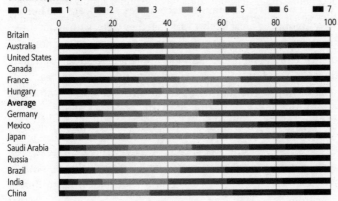

Response v press freedom

Attitude towards free speech†

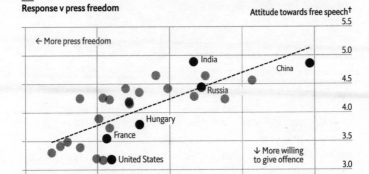

*Survey of 23,004 adults in 28 countries, Dec 23rd 2020 to Jan 8th 2021. Excluding "don't know"
†Weighted-average response to survey question, 0–7
Sources: Ipsos MORI; Reporters Without Borders

to what the Anglosphere would call "political correctness", it may be that, in countries such as China, cautious use of language is required for self-preservation. That might add fuel to conservatives' fire that political correctness could somehow erode democratic norms.

The survey also asked respondents whether they agreed that "culture wars" were dividing their countries. Americans and Indians were among the most likely to say that they were, with about three-fifths agreeing. By contrast, fewer than one-tenth of Japanese and one-fifth of Russians and Germans thought that culture wars were divisive. Yet country-level responses to this question bear little relationship to their attitudes about offensive speech. Although Americans and Britons are similarly exercised about political correctness, just one-third of Britons are concerned about divisive culture wars.

Can video games really be addictive?

It is no fun being a gamer in China – or, at least, less fun that it was. In August 2021 the government announced new rules that restricted the time under-18s can play online games to just an hour a day, on Fridays, Saturdays, Sundays and public holidays. The idea, the censors said, was to "protect the physical and mental health of minors". A particular worry, familiar to parents and gamers themselves, not just to officious Chinese censors, is that at least some video games can be addictive. Can they?

No one doubts that video games can be compelling. Anyone who has played will be familiar with the line of thinking that begins with "just five more minutes" and ends with the sudden realisation that the sun is about to come up. Two decades ago players of "EverQuest", an early massively multiplayer online game, ruefully dubbed their pastime "Evercrack" for its ability to suck them in. The World Health Organisation, for one, takes the analogy seriously. In 2018 it included "gaming disorder" in the 11th revision of its International Classification of Diseases. It defines the disorder as a "pattern of gaming behaviour" in which getting another hit of "Fortnite", for example, becomes more important than other interests and ordinary activities, despite any negative consequences.

But addiction is a complicated idea, and not everyone agrees that video games belong in the same category as caffeine and heroin. One survey published in 2020, by academics at the University of Westminster and Stetson University, in Florida, found that 61% of researchers thought that "pathological gaming" should count as a mental-health disorder, whereas 30% were sceptical (the rest neither agreed nor disagreed). And some of the discussion is coloured by snobbery. After all, "unputdownable" is a term of praise when applied to books.

Rather than worry about categories, economists might prefer to look at incentives. Those faced by game developers have changed over the past couple of decades. Games used to be sold in the same way as carrots or fridges. What users did once they had bought a game – even whether they played it or not – was of little consequence to the developers, who had already made their money. The internet changed that. These days many of the most popular games are played online, and resemble services as much as products. Many cost nothing to play, but rely instead on in-game purchases of decorations or virtual items to make their money. Exchanging a one-off sale for a continuing attempt to extract cash from players incentivises developers to keep their customers playing.

Developers have therefore turned to a variety of psychological tricks to keep players engaged. In a set of pioneering experiments beginning in the 1930s, for instance, the American psychologist B.F. Skinner explored the difference between predictable, random and quasi-random rewards on laboratory rats. That research informs how items, power-ups and the like are doled out in games. Some games are designed to be time-consuming, slowly overwhelming the player with long or difficult tasks, before offering to sell them shortcuts. Others notify players when their friends have bought an item or achieved some goal, subtly playing on envy, status and the fear of missing out. The games themselves use many of the user-experience tricks known as "dark patterns" to nudge players into doing what developers want. The compelling nature of online games is certainly enough to make many people uneasy. But whether hacking the human brain in this way leads to "addiction" is an open question.

Contributors

THE EDITOR WISHES to thank the authors, data journalists and visual journalists who created the explainers and accompanying graphics on which this book is based:

Rachel Ashcroft, Helen Atkinson, Matthew Ball, Aryn Braun, Elise Burr, Geoffrey Carr, Caroline Carter, Philip Coggan, Tim Cross, Rachel Dobbs, Doug Dowson, G. Elliot Morris, Jon Fasman, Glenn Fleishman, Bo Franklin, Daniel Franklin, Alice Fulwood, Neel Ghosh, Amy Hawkins, Michelle Hennessy, Mike Jakeman, Ainslie Johnstone, Shashank Joshi, Margaret Kadifa, Eduin Boater Latimer, Elizabeth Lees, Lea Legraien, Sarah Leo, Joe Lyness, Matt McLean, Claire McQue, Jessie Mathewson, Adam Meara, Oliver Morton, Sacha Nauta, Ore Ogunbiyi, Isobel Owen, Vishnu Padmanabhan, Lloyd Parker, Rosamund Pearce, Lizzy Peet, Arjun Ramani, Daniella Raz, Charles Read, Bill Ridgers, Dan Rosenheck, Lena Schipper, Marie Segger, Alex Selby-Boothroyd, Dolly Setton, Noah Sneider, Sondre Solstad, Matt Steinglass, Ben Throsby, Alex Travelli, Matthew Valencia, Olivia Vane, Hanna Vioque, Eleanor Whitehead, Jonny Williams, Wade Zhou and Dominic Ziegler.

Index

DISCOVER, CLAIM, AND FLOURISH

Reflecting on Your Leadership Journey

Nurturing Leaders. Changing Lives.

HIGHER EDUCATION & MINISTRY
General Board of Higher Education and Ministry
THE UNITED METHODIST CHURCH

Discover, Claim, and Flourish: Reflecting on Your Leadership Journey

Credits
Edited by Kathy Armistead
Designed by Dawn Scott
Illustrations by Jeff Porter and Dawn Scott

DISCOVER, CLAIM, AND FLOURISH
Reflecting on Your Leadership Journey

This leader journal is dedicated to Charles "Ray" Bailey in gratitude and recognition for his years of service to the General Board of Higher Education and Ministry of The United Methodist Church. His careful work as the general editor of this publication reflects his commitment to servant leadership and excellence in ministry.

Charles "Ray" R. Bailey is formerly Associate General Secretary for Strategic Leadership, General Board of Higher Education and Ministry, The United Methodist Church. As a strategic executive mentor and coach, Bailey has built a record of creating effective leadership development programs, honed through years of progressive experience and growth in the US Army (Retired Brigadier General). A trusted advisor to senior leaders, Bailey has a global perspective on culture, values, diversity, and communication that enables him to envision and employ organizational strategies that drive results.

Nurturing Leaders. Changing Lives.

HIGHER EDUCATION & MINISTRY
General Board of Higher Education and Ministry
THE UNITED METHODIST CHURCH

The General Board of Higher Education and Ministry leads and serves The United Methodist Church in the recruitment, preparation, nurture, education, and support of Christian leaders—lay and clergy—for the work of making disciples of Jesus Christ for the transformation of the world. Its vision is that a new generation of Christian leaders will commit boldly to Jesus Christ and be characterized by intellectual excellence, moral integrity, spiritual courage, and holiness of heart and life. The General Board of Higher Education and Ministry of The United Methodist Church serves as an advocate for the intellectual life of the church. The Board's mission embodies the Wesleyan tradition of commitment to the education of laypersons and ordained persons by providing access to higher education for all persons.